THE BEADER'S
Floral

To Ann,

Happy Beading!

Liz Y

and Jill Devon

THE BEADER'S *Floral*

*Stitches, designs, projects and inspiration
for beadwork flowers*

LIZ THORNTON *&* JILL DEVON

A 2beadwrite Book
First edition 2007

First published in the UK in 2007
Published by 2beadwrite ltd
4 Honor Oak Road
London SE23 3SF

www.2beadwrite.com

ISBN 978-0-9556520-0-4

WRITTEN AND EDITED by Liz Thornton & Jill Devon
ILLUSTRATIONS & PHOTOGRAPHY* by Liz Thornton
DESIGNED by Joyce Mason

Printed by Colorprint (Hong Kong)

except for those photographs credited in the Acknowledgements

CONTENTS

INTRODUCTION

FLOWERS ARE A DELIGHTFUL INSPIRATION for creative decoration and we have had enormous enjoyment in devising and presenting these beadwork patterns and also great pleasure in an unexpected and very useful by-product: discovering some new-found additional beading skills!

All of the items in this book are rated by *Fiddly Factor*; a sort of flowery star rating to guide you through which projects to undertake. All of *The Stitch Primer* basic flowers and variations are *Fiddly Factor 1*. That means that you should start here – with whichever stitch or style that you like, and practice a bit until you feel comfortable with the stitch. Then try the named flower in that stitch and maybe even the project before you tackle some of the other named flowers. You will also find that many of the flowers in other sections of the book refer back to this *Primer*.

THE STITCH PRIMER introduces the stitches that we think have the greatest potential to create these beautiful flowers. Each stitch (there are four: *Herringbone*, *Brick*, *Square* and *Peyote*) starts with a basic flower and then there are several variations so that you can explore the potential of the stitches and see that by just subtle variations in bead placement or manipulation, or a different number of petals, or a combination of two or more styles, you will be able to vary the appearance of the flowers to create a veritable potpourri of blossoms.

THE FLOWER COLLECTION features more of our favourite flowers (they are presented in order of *Fiddly Factor* but remember that everybody takes to different stitches in different ways, so please don't think if you are having trouble with a particular one that you won't be able to do some of the others). Who could not adore these sweet daffodils and fuchsias, or want to try those intricate columbines or orchids? You will be amazed at how quickly you will be able to grow your flowers, and what satisfaction and delight they will bring!

BUDS & GREENERY contains all the little extras – lots of small and pretty floral motifs such as leaves, sepals, tendrils, buds, tiny flowers and berries which can be added to all of your projects to create a lush and a more decorative effect. This is also the place to find different stamen ideas to put in the centres of your flowers to finish and fix them to perfection. The *Fiddly Factor* ranges from 1 to 3 and the styles are varied so there will be plenty of choices and challenges.

■ **FLOWERY BRAIDS** include a wealth of patterns for simple little chains and necklaces that look lovely on their own or would be equally charming as the base for other projects or as edging for cushions or cardigans. They are all very simple (with a *Fiddly Factor* of either 1 or 2) and quick and easy to produce.

■ **THE PROJECTS** then bring all these designs and ideas together: having made a treasure trove of flowers you may now want to incorporate them into a necklace or bracelet or a brooch (and here the *Fiddly Factor* relates to the making of the overall project itself rather than to the component braid or flower that is used for it). So in a few of the *Projects* (such as *Blossom, Heartsease* and *Posy Necklaces*) we have combined a Braid and a Flower from the preceding sections to give you some ideas of how to put the pieces together. In most instances the flowers are completely interchangeable; and that should provide you with a wealth of other possibilities. We have also included a new flower and project, the *Anemone Corsage*, which is on a larger scale and two charts for you to bead lovely floral pictures.

■ **THE ALBUM** is the final section, and here we have provided a gallery to showcase some more of our own floral beadwork projects which we hope will give you further inspiration for using beadwork around the home and in jewellery and textile decoration.

Creating the flowers in *The Beaders Floral* will provide you with a treasure trove of decorative items that you will be able to use for countless projects; and will give you many rewarding hours contemplating your own floral designs. Indeed, as we were putting this book together so many more flowers demanded to be beaded – sweet peas, fritillarias, hellebores, alliums – that we could have gone on for ever! But we hope that the selection that we have made (in the flowers and in the projects) offers a balance of styles and a range of challenges; and, in the process, that we have sewn the seeds of creative beading which will make you eager to explore the potential and the pleasures of beadwork.

TIPS & TECHNIQUES

*N*OT ALL BEADS ARE BORN EQUAL. When you start to work the flowers described on the following pages you will really notice the difference if you use better quality beads. We have used Japanese beads – either Miyuki or Toho who both make the best quality beads with fine, even shapes. If you have even just one bead that is a slightly different shape to the others you will find it quite noticeable and if there are several your lovely flower may start to look like a weed! In the shopping lists if we have mentioned that you need 'a few' beads but not given the amount then we are presuming that you may already have some beads that are suitable. If not you will need to buy a minimum quantity (usually 5 or 10g). You will notice in some instances that we have suggested cylinder beads; you could choose Delica, Treasures or Aikos.

We have also used best quality Swarovski crystals throughout as the accent beads – but our motives in this instance were not quite so pure – because they are so irresistibly pretty, twinkly and in such gorgeous colours. You, of course, don't have to, other beads could be substituted; but we imagine you'll be glad of any excuse to get those crystals out!

Work with whatever beading needle you feel comfortable with (size 10 is the easiest to thread) but change to a finer needle when the going gets tight. Do not force a needle through a bead - you risk breaking both.

The thread that we have used is Nymo or C-lon. For these projects they have just the right amount of stretch and strength to enable us to get that needle into a very tight spot, and also to keep the tension quite firm.

Don't use too long a thread when going through the same bead(s) lots of times, especially if using size 14/15s. It will just fray and get thick and useless with lots of stray fibres. (Protecting your thread with a conditioner really helps, but it cannot work miracles!) But do make sure to leave a tail of at least 20 cm (8") when starting any of the items in this book. Not only is it important to have sufficient thread to neaten off later, but it is also really useful to have something to hang on to whilst working, for convenience and for tension – particularly in the early stages.

If you need to start a new thread in the middle of your work; either weave in a new length, changing direction lots of times, or hold both old and new ends together and tie with an overhand knot. (Don't wait until the last minute to add a new thread. It's much easier to attach and weave in if there is plenty of thread to work with.) If you are working in *Brick Stitch* you will not want the knot in the way, so use a pair of tweezers or a needle to guide the knot into a position where it will not be troublesome. Leave the spare ends until you have finished and then weave in a little before cutting. Always follow the particular thread path when needling through the work.

There is very little room in the flower to allow finishing ends to be woven in satisfactorily; therefore always knot the thread at the end to finish, and possibly earlier as well. If your needle will not pass through a bead because there is a knot in the way, then gently pull on the thread to ease it out of the way whilst you push the needle through.

If, when working, you feel a knot forming, immediately loosen and remove it. Do not think it will go away if you ignore it or worse still, disappear if you pull it tight – it will only get worse and leave you very frustrated!

Fine tweezers are extremely useful for removing unwanted knots. If your thread does keep kinking into knots then allow the thread to relax and unwind and ease and condition it with Thread Heaven (or Beeswax if you want a stiffer thread).

Be careful not to pierce the already worked thread with your needle. The problem will be minimised if you keep the tension even and always try to put the needle through the top of the bead hole.

If you are new to beadwork and have not beaded on this small scale before you may find it easier to practice first by working each row in a different colour so that you can see how the pattern builds up and where to place your beads. The diagrams in *The Stitch Primer* are also colour coded row by row. You may also like to count out the correct amount and size of beads required for each row so that you will know if you are working correctly.

And if you are not sure what size beads to start working with, then by all means begin with a bigger size (seed 11 or even 8) until you are feeling comfortable with the stitch. We have made samples in *The Stitch Primer* in different sized beads and you will see that the flowers all look great whatever size you choose.

As we have mentioned in the *Introduction*, all the patterns have a *Fiddly Factor* rating and the majority of them are from 1 - 3 which is easily accessible by most. A *Fiddly Factor* of 4, however, is more of a challenge; so please do not attempt them until you have gained confidence on other pieces and are well armed with the following weapons: very fine needles and thread, light, magnifier, tweezers, thread conditioner, (and perhaps a bottle of wine). Happy Beading!

PART 1

THE STITCH PRIMER

We have chosen four stitches to make the flowers. With each stitch, start with the basic version and work through a few of the variations. You will soon see that by just subtle changes in bead placement or manipulation, or a combination of different stitches, you will be able to vary the appearance of the flowers to create a veritable potpourri of blossoms.

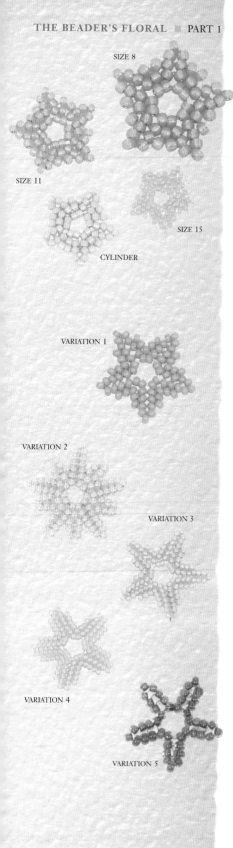

SIZE 8

SIZE 11

CYLINDER

SIZE 15

VARIATION 1

VARIATION 2

VARIATION 3

VARIATION 4

VARIATION 5

Herringbone Stitch Daisy Flowers

Circular Herringbone Stitch makes good multi-petalled flowers or any star-shaped flowers where the petal size decreases towards the tip such as daisies. It is very useful to combine with other stitches once the basic structure is started, and makes very good tubes for wonderful trumpet flowers, such as daturas or dainty bluebells and showy morning glories.

Basic Circular Herringbone Stitch Flower

General note

■ With *Circular Herringbone* all the petals are made at the same time, building up row on row. It is important to 'step up' at the end of each row before you can work the next. Before you start, remember to look at the *Tips and Techniques Section* on *pages 8 & 9*

Foundation

F Pick up 10 beads and go through all the beads again to turn them into a circle. Do not knot. (But if this is your very first flower then tie the two ends of thread together to make it easier to work.)

Petals

1 Pass through the 1st bead, * pick up 2 and pass through the next two beads. Continue around, repeating from *. Make sure that each new pair of beads sits correctly by pushing them down with your thumb and pulling the thread tight so that the bead holes face upwards.

This is how the beads should sit

At the end of the row, pass up into the 1st new bead added ready to start the next row, ie 'step up'.

2 * Pick up 2 and pass down into the 2nd new bead of the previous row (this is the rib). Pick up 1 and pass up into the next rib. Continue around, repeating from *. 'Step up' as before at the end of the row.

3 Place 3 beads on to each rib instead of 2 (to make a picot). Pick up 2 beads between each rib instead of 1.

Work back down to the tail thread and knot, then weave in and bury ends.

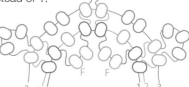

In working any of the *Variations*, remember to 'step up' at the end of each row.

Variation 1

F, 1 & 2 Work as Rows F, 1 & 2 from the *Basic Circular Herringbone Flower*.

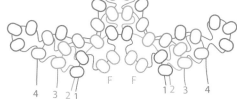

3 * Place 2 beads on to the rib, then pick up 1 and pass through the new central bead (between the ribs). Pick up 1 and pass up into the next rib. Continue around, repeating from *.

4 * Add 3 on to the rib (to make a picot), then pick up 1 and pass down through the 1st side bead and the original central bead and then up through the next side bead (so that you are following the thread path). Pick up 1 and pass up into the rib. Continue around, repeating from *.

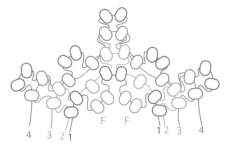

❖❖❖

Variation 2

F, 1 & 2 Work as Rows F, 1 & 2 from the *Basic Circular Herringbone Flower*.

3 Place 2 beads on to the rib and 2 beads between each rib. Continue around.

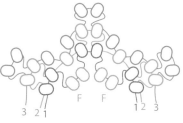

4 * Place 2 beads on to the rib. Follow the thread path to the 1st new bead just added in Row 3 and pick up 2. Pass down into the next bead and up to the top of the next rib. This is effectively starting another set of ribs. Continue around, repeating from *.

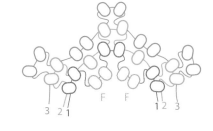

5 * Place 3 beads on to the rib. Follow the thread path down and then up into the next rib to avoid unsightly threads and add 3. Again follow the thread path down and then up to the top of the next rib. Continue around, repeating from *. (In the diagram, the thread path for this row is only shown at the top of the ribs, not along the sides.)

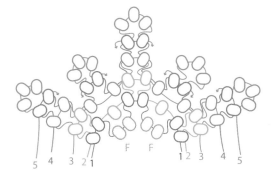

Variation 3

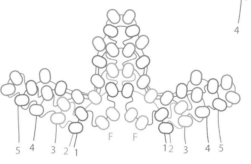

F, 1 & 2 Work as Rows F, 1 & 2 from the *Basic Circular Herringbone Flower*.

3 * Place 2 beads on to the rib, then pick up 1 and pass through the new central bead (between the ribs). Pick up 1 and pass up into the next rib ready to continue around, repeating from *.

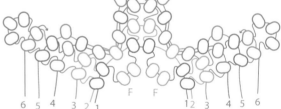

4 * Place 2 on to the rib. Then pick up 1 and pass down through the 1st side bead and the original central bead and then up through the next side bead (so that you are following the thread path). Pick up 1 and pass up into the rib. Continue around, repeating from *.

5 * Place 2 beads on to the rib. Then pick up 1 and pass down into the 1st side bead and then follow the thread path down and then up. Pick up 1 and pass into the rib. Continue around, repeating from *.

6 * Place 3 beads on to the rib and follow the thread path to the next rib (this will help to strengthen the petals). Continue around, repeating from *. (In the diagram, the thread path for this row is only shown at the top of the ribs, not along the sides.)

◆◆◆

Variation 4

F, 1 & 2 Work as Rows F, 1 & 2 from the *Basic Circular Herringbone Flower*.

3 * Place 2 beads on to the rib, then pick up 1 and pass through the new central bead (between the rib).

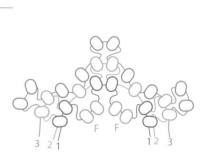

Pick up 1 and pass up into the next rib ready to continue around, repeating from *.

4 * Place 2 on to the rib. Then pick up 1 and pass down through the 1st side bead and the original central bead and then up through the next side bead (so that you are following the thread path). Pick up 1 and pass up into the rib. Continue around, repeating from *.

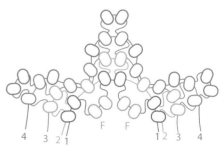

5 * Place 2 beads on to the rib. Then pick up 1 and pass down into the 1st side bead and then follow the thread path down and then up. Pick up 1 and pass into the rib. Continue around, repeating from *.

6 * Place 2 beads on to the rib. Then pick up 1 and pass down into the 1st side bead and then follow the thread path down and then up. Pick up 1 and pass into the rib. Continue around, repeating from *. (In the diagram, the thread path for this row is only shown at the top of the ribs, not along the sides.)

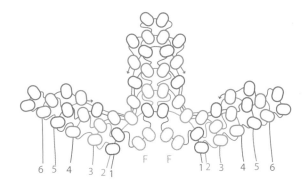

Variation 5

F & 1 Work as Rows F & 1 from the *Basic Circular Herringbone Flower*.

2 * Pick up 2 beads and pass down into the Foundation Row to keep the petals separate. Pass up into the next rib. Continue around, repeating from *.

3 Place 3 on to the rib and follow the thread path as before to the top of the next rib. Continue around, repeating from *. (In the diagram, the thread path for this row is only shown at the top of the ribs, not along the sides.)

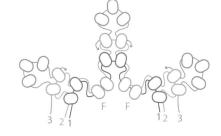

Tip

All of these petals are symmetrical: so if at any time you are not sure which bead to needle into, check how you have worked the other petals.

Lily HERRINGBONE STITCH

Cultivated for over 3000 years, these beautiful flowers symbolise purity and innocence. There are many varieties and shapes of flower, which may be like a trumpet, a funnel, a star or a turks cap.

These gorgeous Stargazer Lilies are very open and their six petals curve back only slightly to reveal the stamens. They are made in Tubular and Circular Herringbone Stitch and would look equally lovely in any of the smaller seed bead sizes.

FIDDLY FACTOR

SHOPPING LIST

seed beads
(any size 10 -15)
a few small bugles
for the stamens

Foundation

F Pick up 6 beads and go through all the beads again to turn them into a circle. Do not knot.

Petals

1 Work as Row 1 from the *Basic Herringbone Daisy Flower* on *page 12.*

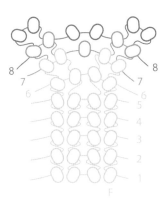

2 * Pick up 2 and pass down into the bead below and up the adjacent bead. Continue around, repeating from *. Step up at the end of the row.

3 - 6 Repeat Row 2.

7 Work as Row 2 from the *Basic Herringbone Daisy Flower* on *page 12.*

8 Place 2 beads on to the rib and 2 beads between each rib.

9 * Place 2 beads on to the rib and pick up 1 bead.
Pass through the 1st of the 2 new beads added on to the previous row and pick up 4.
Pass down into the next new bead, pick up 1 and pass up into the next rib.

Continue around, repeating from * (i.e. 2 on an old rib, 4 on the new rib, and 1 between each).

10 * Place 2 beads on to the rib. Then pick up 1 and pass down into the new central bead between the ribs. Pick up 1 and pass up into the top bead of the next rib ready to continue around, repeating from *.

11 * Place 2 beads on to the rib. Then pick up 1 and pass down through the 1st side bead and the original central bead and then up through the next side bead (so that you are following the thread path). Pick up 1 and pass up into the rib. Continue around, repeating from *.

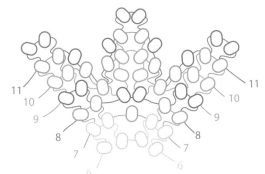

12 Repeat Row 11 again.

13 Place 3 on to the rib and 1 on each side (as above, following the thread path). Continue around.

14 Finally, pass the needle all the way around the outside edge of the petals. (The central bead will be quite full by now – do not force the needle through, but rather go down to a smaller needle size.)
Pull gently after each petal and shape the beads so that the petals curve back slightly along their edges.

Stamens

Work back to the inside of the tube to make the stamens. * Pick up 2 bugles and a seed bead, turn and pass back through the bugles into the tube. Bring the needle out to the side of the first stamen and repeat from * twice.

Posy Necklace

This charming necklace is made with strands of Daisy Chains (that would also look very pretty on their own) combined with a beaded bead that showcases a posy of lilies. The beaded bead is perfectly interchangeable (as long as the clasp is small enough – a toggle would work well) so that you could have a variety of posies to suit your mood.

To make the Necklace

1 Using the M and C seed beads, make 5 strands of *Daisy Chain* from the instructions on *page 99*, with the daisies randomly interspersed so that they do not all occur together. Pass all the threads through a bicone crystal and fasten the clasp on. Repeat for the other end.

To make the Posy Beaded Bead

Brick Stitch Base

1 Foundation Row: Pick up 3D and pass back down the 1st D, but in the opposite direction (towards the tail). Leave a long tail and knot the two threads together. Pick up 1D and pass up through 1 of the beads above (it doesn't matter which). Pick up another D and pass down through the 4th D (the bead just added). Continue in this zig zag manner until there are 32 beads in total – 16 on top and 16 below.

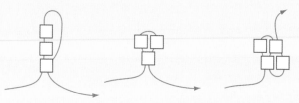

2 Now work in *Brick Stitch* (first turn the work and hold it so that you are working from left to right): pick up 2D and pass the needle under the loop of thread joining the beads in the Foundation Row.
Go back up through the 2nd D. Pull gently so that the 2 beads stand side by side on top of the base row.

Add 1D and pass the needle through the next loop of thread available, and then back up through the D.
Repeat all the way along.

Turn and repeat for another 2 rows.

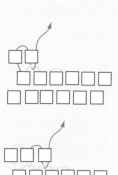

FIDDLY FACTOR
❀❀ ❀❀

SHOPPING LIST

For the Necklace:
25g seed bead size 11 main colour M
10g seed bead size 11 contrast colour C
2 x 5mm Swarovski bicone crystals
toggle clasp

For the Beaded Bead:
5g cylinders main colour D
a few cylinders lighter toning colour L
5g seed bead size 15 to match
the light cylinders T
1 x 8mm Swarovski round crystal
3 x 3mm or 4mm Swarovski
bicone crystals
3 Lilies in toning colours, preferably in
different sizes beads such as 11 and
15 seed beads and cylinders

Change to L beads and work one row, and then return to the D beads for 5 rows.

Bend the strip around so that the two ends meet and sew through the beads that slot into one another to form a tube.

Embellishment

1 With the needle exiting from a bead on the edge of the tube, pass the needle down the next edge bead so that it is pointing towards the centre of the tube. * Pick up 3D and pass straight down into the bead on the third row (on the same line of beadwork). Pass sideways into the adjacent bead.

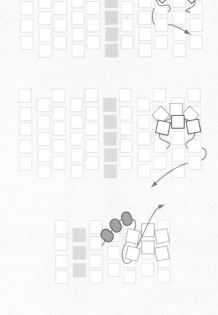

Pick up 3D and pass straight up into the edge row again. Pass sideways into the next edge bead and repeat from* all the way around.
Weave through to the other edge of the tube and repeat the process to add a line of picots on that side.

2 Weave through to one of the rows of *Brick Stitch* adjacent to the row of L beads, pointing towards the edging of picots already made. Pick up 3T and pass down the nearest bead of the picot which is sitting on the same line of beadwork. Pass the needle up the adjacent bead of the next picot (you don't need to go into the base tube). Pick up 3T and pass into the next bead on the row of *Brick Stitch* next to the L beads. Continue all the way around in the same manner, and then repeat for the other side of the tube.

Adding the Flowers

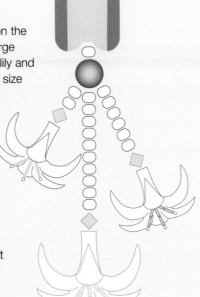

Pass the needle through to any L bead on the beaded bead and pick up 1M and the large crystal. * Pick up 10M, a small crystal, a lily and enough M or T beads (depending on the size of the flower) to pass through it's throat, 1M and then turn and pass back all the way up into the beaded bead. Tug gently to check that the lily is secure. If not, you may have to catch a thread or two onto the flower itself. Catch the thread onto the beaded bead and turn and go back through the 1M and large crystal. Repeat from * with the rest of the flowers, making the stem length quite different in each case so that they all hang nicely.

Tip

Don't forget to add the stamens to the lilies before you attach them to the beaded bead. And you can, of course, make them more flamboyant than we have.

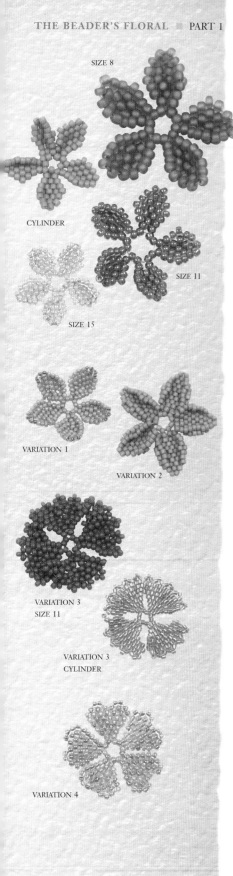

SIZE 8

CYLINDER

SIZE 11

SIZE 15

VARIATION 1

VARIATION 2

VARIATION 3
SIZE 11

VARIATION 3
CYLINDER

VARIATION 4

Brick Stitch Blossom Flowers

Brick Stitch from a circular foundation makes wonderful blossom style flowers, and by manipulating and shaping the individual petals all sorts of gorgeous blooms can be made – such as pansies and iris. In addition, by combining Tubular Herringbone with Brick Stitch such delights as snowdrops and fuchsias can be created.

General notes

■ Once you have made the two base rows each petal is worked separately. Before you start, remember to look at the *Tips and Techniques Section* on *pages 8 & 9*.

■ In our *Brick Stitch* instructions, the first stitch of a row will always start with 2 beads on to the loop (this hides the thread) whether or not you are increasing or decreasing or remaining the same. You will need to do this or the patterns will not work out correctly.

■ When decreasing at the beginning of a row in *Brick Stitch*, the first bead frequently sits a little drunkenly. We always work the 2 beads on the first loop first in *Square Stitch* and then again in *Brick Stitch* (*not shown again in later diagrams*).

Basic Brick Stitch Flower

Foundation

F Pick up 10 beads and go through all the beads again to turn them into a circle. Do not knot. (But if this is your very first flower then tie the two ends of thread together to make it easier to work.)

Petals

1 Pass through the 1st bead, * pick up 2 and pass down through the next two beads. Continue around, repeating from *. Make sure that each new pair of beads sits correctly by pushing them down with your thumb and pulling the thread tight so that the bead holes face upwards.

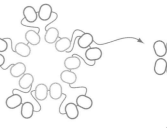

This is how the beads should sit.

At the end of the row, pass up into the 1st new bead added ready to start the next row, ie 'step up'.

Now work on one petal at a time.

2 Pick up 2 beads and pass the needle under the thread joining the top of the beads in Row 1 and back up through the 2nd bead. Pull gently so that the two beads sit correctly. Pick up 1 bead and pass the needle under the same thread as previously and back up through the bead just added. Jiggle the three beads so that they sit correctly. (You should have 3 beads on this row) Turn.

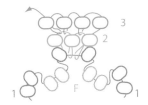

3 Pick up 2 beads on to the 1st loop, and two beads on to the 2nd loop (worked individually) (total 4 beads). Turn.

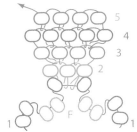

4 Pick up 2 beads on to the 1st loop, 1 on to the 2nd loop, and 2 on to the 3rd loop (total 5 beads). Turn.

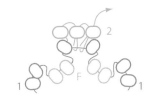

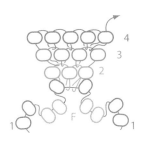

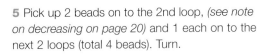

5 Pick up 2 beads on to the 2nd loop, *(see note on decreasing on page 20)* and 1 each on to the next 2 loops (total 4 beads). Turn.

6 Pick up 2 beads on to the 2nd loop and 1 on to the 3rd loop (total 3 beads). Turn.

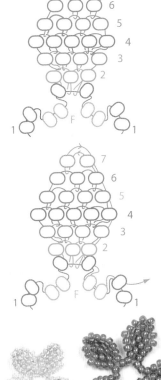

7 Pick up 2 beads on to the 2nd loop (total 2 beads).

Pass the needle down through the 1st bead and then needle all the way down the outside edge and into the F Row (pulling very gently to introduce a little shaping into the petal) and up the next bead on Row 1 ready to start another petal.

Continue as above all the way around each of the five petals.

If you wish to add more shaping to the finished flower then needle all the way around the outside edge of each petal, pulling very gently.

Work back to the tail thread and knot again, then weave in and bury ends.

Variation 1

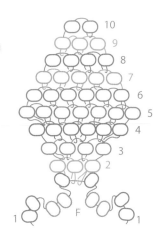

F, 1, 2 & 3 Work as Rows F, 1, 2 & 3 from the *Basic Brick Stitch Flower.*

4 Pick up 2 beads on to the 1st loop, 2 on to the 2nd loop, and 2 on to the 3rd loop (total 6 beads).

5 Pick up 2 beads on to the 1st loop, 1 each on to the next 3, and 2 on to the last (total 7 beads).

6, 7, 8, 9 & 10 Decrease by 1 bead at the beginning of each row.

Pass the needle down through the last bead and then needle all the way down the outside edge and into the F Row (pulling very gently to introduce a little shaping into the petal) and up the next bead on Row 1 ready to start another petal.

Continue as above all the way around for each of the five petals. If you wish to add more shaping to the finished flower then needle all the way around the outside edge of each petal, pulling very gently.

◆◆◆

Variation 2

F & 1 Work as Rows F & 1 from the *Basic Brick Stitch Flower.*

1A *Ladder Stitch* an additional bead either side of the two beads already in position:

Pick up 1 bead and pass the needle back through the 1st bead in the same direction. Needle around again for strength. Pass through the next bead and back through the previous bead again. Pass back into the 2nd bead, pick up 1 and pass through the 2nd bead again and back up the new bead.

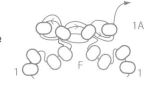

2 Pick up 2 beads on to the 1st loop, 2 on to the 2nd loop, and 2 on to the 3rd loop (total 6 beads).

3, 4 & 5 Increase by 1 bead at the end of each row (total 9 beads).

6, 7 & 8 Decrease by 1 bead at each beginning of row (total 6 beads).

9 Pick up 2 beads on to the 3rd loop (hook through the 2nd loop) and 1 bead on to the 4th (total 3 beads). Turn.

Detail showing the beginning of Row 9

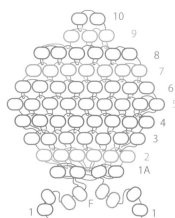

10 Pick up 2 beads on to the 2nd loop (total 2 beads).

Pass the needle down through the last bead and then needle all the way down the outside edge and into the F Row (pulling very gently to introduce a little shaping into the petal) and up the next bead on Row 1 ready to start another petal.

Continue as above all the way around for each of the five petals. If you wish to add more shaping to the finished flower then needle all the way around the outside edge of each petal, pulling very gently.

Variation 3

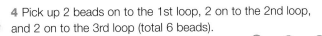

F Pick up 8 beads and turn into a circle. Knot.

1, 2 & 3 Work as Rows 1, 2 & 3 from the *Basic Brick Stitch Flower*.

4 Pick up 2 beads on to the 1st loop, 2 on to the 2nd loop, and 2 on to the 3rd loop (total 6 beads).

5 Pick up 2 beads on to each loop (total 10 beads).

6 Increase by 1 bead at the end of the row (total 11 beads).

7 Decrease by 1 bead at the beginning of the row (total 10 beads).

8 Picot along this row: * pick up 3 beads and pass the needle down the next bead of the row below. Pass up into the next bead and pick up 3. Repeat from * across the row.

Pass the needle down through the last bead and then needle all the way down the outside edge and into the F Row (pulling very gently to introduce a little shaping into the petal) and up the next bead on Row 1 ready to start another petal.

Continue as above all the way around for each of the four petals.

Variation 4

F, 1, 2, 3 & 4 Work as Rows F, 1, 2, 3 & 4 from the *Basic Brick Stitch Flower*.

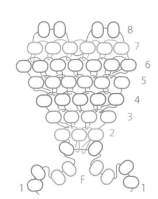

5 Pick up 2 beads on to the 1st loop, 1 each on to the next 2, and 2 on to the last (total 6 beads).

6 Pick up 2 beads on to the 1st loop, 1 each on the next 3, and 2 on to the last (total 7 beads).

7 Decrease by 1 bead at the beginning of the row (total 6 beads).

8 Pick up 2 beads and pass down into the 3rd bead. Pass up the 4th bead, pick up 2 and pass down the last bead.

Needle all the way down the outside edge and into the F Row (pulling very gently to introduce a little shaping into the petal) and up the next bead on Row 1 ready to start another petal.

Continue as above all the way around for each of the five petals.

Pansy BRICK STITCH

This most endearing of traditional garden flowers is derived from the wildflower Heartsease (viola tricolour), whilst its name is from the French 'pensée' (thought).

These exquisite Brick Stitch Pansies are quite fiddly to make and should not be attempted until you have completed some of the other Brick Stitch flowers – in particular Variation 2. They look equally beautiful in any of the smaller seed bead sizes (10 – 15) or in cylinders, but if you choose the tiny size 15s try to obtain the finest possible thread.

The flowers include different colours to show off their faces which are marked in the petal charts, but for ease of understanding, the instructions do not mention any colours. When you have finished the two base rows, needle to A and then work each petal separately in the sequence described.

When you have completed all of the petals (1 central petal A, 2 side petals B, and 2 top petals C) manipulate them as in the diagram and sew a few stitches to fix them into place if you wish.

FIDDLY FACTOR

SHOPPING LIST

seed beads
(any size 10 -15) or
cylinder beads with a few
additional beads in two
contrasting colours

Foundation

Work as Rows F & 1 from the *Basic Brick Stitch Flower*, placing the colours as shown.
Needle to A.

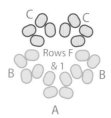

Central Petal A

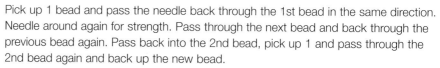

1a *Ladder Stitch* an additional bead either side of the two beads already in position:

Pick up 1 bead and pass the needle back through the 1st bead in the same direction. Needle around again for strength. Pass through the next bead and back through the previous bead again. Pass back into the 2nd bead, pick up 1 and pass through the 2nd bead again and back up the new bead.

2 Pick up 2 beads on to the 1st loop, 2 on to the 2nd loop, and 2 on to the 3rd loop (total 6 beads).

3 Pick up 2 beads on to the 1st loop, 1 each on to the next 3, and 2 on to the last (total 7 beads).

4 Pick up 2 beads on to the 1st loop, 1 each on to the next 4, and 2 on to the last (total 8 beads).

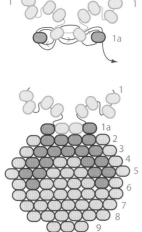

5 Pick up 2 beads on to the 1st loop, 1 each on to the next 5, and 2 on to the last (total 9 beads).

6 Decrease by 1 bead at the beginning of the row i.e. into 2nd available loop, but pick up 4 beads instead of 2 and work in *2-drop* all the way along (2 beads per stitch making the equivalent of two identical rows of 8 beads, or 8 stacks – take a look at the Tip Box on *page 59).*

7 & 8 Working again in regular *Brick Stitch* decrease by 1 bead at the beginning of each row (total 7, then 6 beads).

9 Pick up 2 beads on to the 3rd loop (hook through the 2nd loop) and 1 bead on to the 4th (total 3 beads).

Needle through to the next petal, Side Petal B

Side Petal B

1a Work as Row 1a of Central Petal A.

2 Pick up 2 beads on to the 1st loop, 1 on to the 2nd loop, and 2 on to the 3rd loop (total 5 beads).

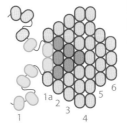

3 Pick up 2 beads on to the 1st loop, 1 each on to the next 2 and 2 on to the 4th loop (total 6 beads).

4 Working in *2-drop*, pick up 4 beads on to the 1st loop, 2 each on to the next 3, and 4 on to the last (2 beads per stitch making the equivalent of two identical rows of 7 beads).

5 Working again in regular *Brick Stitch*, pick up 2 beads on to the 3rd loop and 1 each on to the next 2 (total 4 beads).

6 Pick up 2 beads on to the 2nd loop and 1 on to the 3rd loop (total 3 beads).

Needle through to the next petal, Top Petal C

Top Petal C continues overleaf

Top Petal C

1a *Ladder Stitch* an additional 2 beads either side of the two beads already in position. Be sure to reinforce those two original beads.

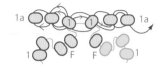

1b Hook through the top thread to exit the bottom of the end bead. Pick up 2 beads on to the 2nd loop and *Brick Stitch* into position underneath.
Needle back to Row 1a and weave through to the opposite end, exiting at the bottom of the last bead (*see diagram at right*).
Repeat the two beads underneath. Exit upwards at the end bead of Row 1a.

2 Pick up 2 beads on to the 1st loop, 1 each on to the next 3, and 2 on to the last loop (total 7 beads).

3 Working in *2-drop*, pick up 4 beads on to the 1st loop, 2 each on to the next 4, and 4 on to the last (2 beads per stitch making the equivalent of two identical rows of 8 beads).

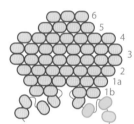

4 Working again in regular *Brick Stitch* decrease by 1 bead at the beginning of the row (total 7 beads).

5 Pick up 2 beads on to the 3rd loop and 1 each on to the next 2 (total 4 beads).

6 Pick up 2 beads on to the 2nd loop and 1 on to the 3rd loop (total 3 beads).

cylinder

Needle through to the next petal, Top Petal C and repeat.

Size 11

Needle through to the next petal, Side Petal B and repeat.

Work back to the tail thread and knot. Manipulate the petals so that they sit correctly, and then needle around the Foundation Row, as many times as possible to strengthen whilst catching the petals in position.

Size 15

Tip

Sew the individual petals of the pansies into place first – with the petals overlapping correctly – before you place them onto your project. Then attach each flower through the centre of the pansy, with or without a central bead, and also through the petals in one or two places if they need to sit in a certain direction.

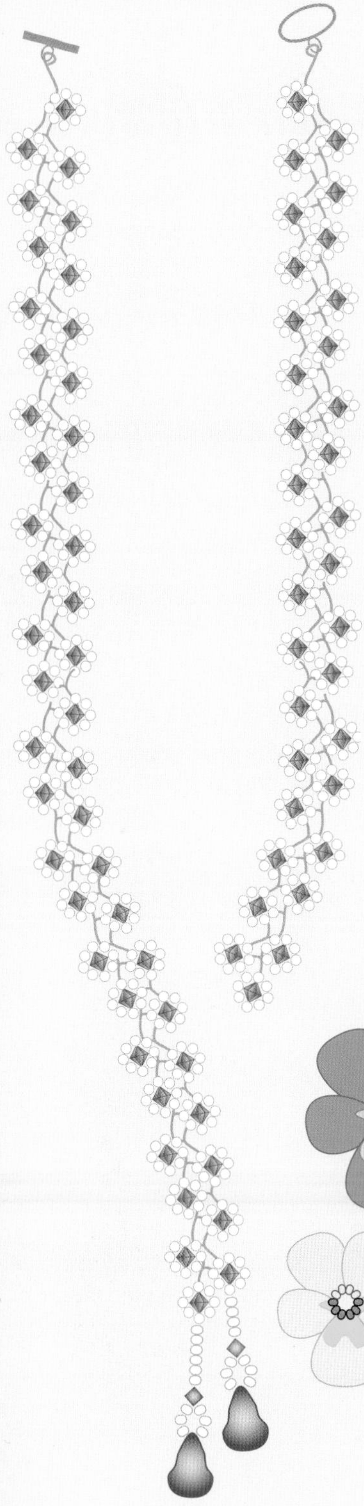

Heartsease Necklace

This pretty necklace has a very old-fashioned, evocative aura about it – possibly related to the flowers themselves and to the delicate braid necklace which twists and turns delightfully; but also because of the subtle colour used here and the refined baroque crystal drops. It is made using the Flower Blossom Braid and three of the pansies. It would also look lovely with other patterns from the Flowery Braids Section or with different flowers as the focal point.

FIDDLY FACTOR

Using the M and C beads with the tiny crystals for the centre beads, make two *Flower Blossom Braids* – one of 25 cms (10") and one of 30 cms (12") – from the pattern on *page 95*. With the blossoms on the braids facing downwards, attach a clasp to the top stalk ends.

Sew the shorter braid to the longer one so that 5 cms (2") of the longer braid fall in a single, central fringe. At the end of the fringe, pick up 6M, a small crystal, 3M, the crystal drop, 3M and back up through the small crystal and 6M. Pass around the blossom and back up and around to exit from the blossom above. Pick up 4M, a small crystal, 3M, the crystal drop, 3M and back up through the small crystal and 4M.

Position the three pansies at the junction of the two braids and sew into place.

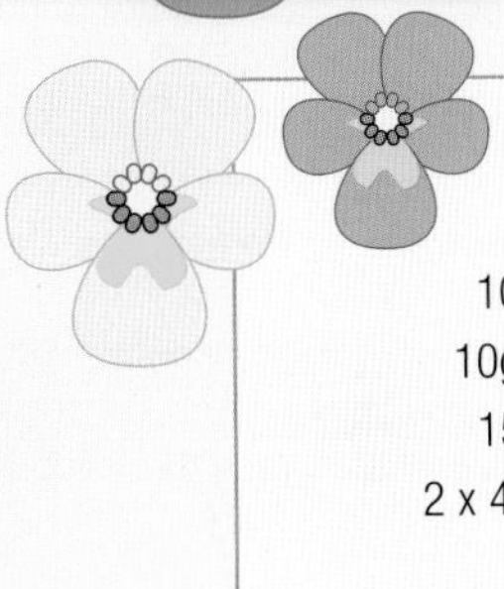

SHOPPING LIST

For the necklace:

10g seed bead size 11 main colour M

10g seed bead size 11 contrast colour C

150 x 3mm Swarovski bicone crystals

2 x 4mm Swarovski bicone or round crystals

2 x Swarovski baroque drops

toggle clasp

3 Pansies in toning colours, preferably in different sized beads such as seed beads 11, 15 and cylinders

27

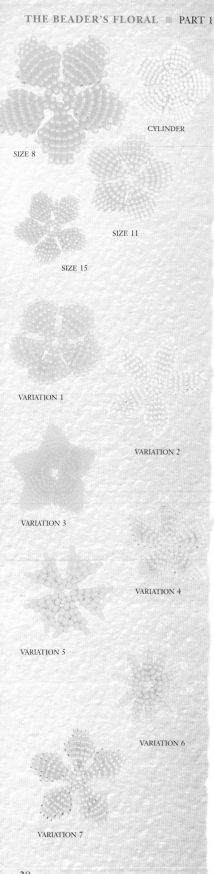

CYLINDER

SIZE 8

SIZE 11

SIZE 15

VARIATION 1

VARIATION 2

VARIATION 3

VARIATION 4

VARIATION 5

VARIATION 6

VARIATION 7

Square Stitch Cupped Flowers

The gently cupped petals of our Square Stitch flowers bring to mind so many flowers such as primulas, roses, buttercups, poppies and geraniums. The stitch is easy to do and to shape. We have given you some general instructions at the beginning of this section to avoid too much repetition in the individual flowers. Read them through carefully first – there are many different ways to shape with this stitch and the way we have chosen to work here may not be the method you are familiar with.

General notes

■ Once you have made the two base rows each petal is worked separately. Before you start, remember to look at the *Tips and Techniques Section* on *pages 8 & 9*.

■ *Square Stitch* uses a lot of thread and you are unlikely to complete a flower with just one length. To join in a new length, weave the thread through the beadwork, turning several times as you go (the beadwork is very dense, so there is no need to make any knots).

■ The thread will show, so use a colour that matches your beads as closely as possible.

■ The holes of the beads get quite full, so choose beads with good holes and use the finest grade of thread available to you.

■ At the beginning of each row, the thread is always pointing outwards from the petal.

To work Square Stitch

Having first worked the 2 base rows of the Foundation as described for each flower on the following pages, pick up 1 bead, go through the bead the thread is coming from, from the opposite side; go through the new bead again *(Diagram 1)*. Repeat across the row *(Diagram 2)*.

The next row is worked in the opposite direction across the beads just added, so the stitching is reversed *(Diagrams 3 & 4)*.

Diag 1   Diag 2   Diag 3   Diag 4

Decreasing in Square Stitch

On the edge at the beginning of a row, weave to the correct position by going through the 2 beads on the edge of the row below, turn and go through the second to last bead of the current row. *(Diagram 5)*
Pick up the first bead of the new row and stitch in place. *(Diagram 6)*

Diag 5

Diag 6

On the edge at the end of a row, simply turn before the final bead.

In the course of a row, EITHER stitch 1 bead on to 2 beads of the row below OR simply miss a bead in the row below.

To place the decrease in the centre of a row:

- over a row which has an even number of beads, stitch 1 bead on to the central 2 beads of the row below.

- over a row which has an odd number of beads, miss the bead in the centre of the row.

When you decrease in the centre of a row, you will find that the centre bead of the previous row will be forced out of line and the petal will begin to curve. When working a flower, make sure to encourage all its petals to curve in the same direction.

◆◆◆

Increasing in Square Stitch

Stitch 2 beads on to 1 bead of the previous row and go through both new beads again. *(Diagram 7)*

Diag 7

When increasing in the middle of a row which has an even number of beads: work half the row straight, pick up 2 beads and stitch them on to the next bead, but only go through the 2nd of the new beads a second time – this ensures that the first bead sits centrally in the row *(Diagram 8)*.

Diag 8

Tip

When working in *Square Stitch*, just one bead more or less in a row can make a surprising difference to the shape of the beadwork. On occasion we have placed a decrease row immediately next to an increase row and this produces the sharpest shifts. If you prefer to soften the shaping, you can do so by adding one or two straight rows between the increase and decrease rows. We will remind you of this from time to time in later instructions where it seems particularly appropriate.

Basic Square Stitch Flower

Foundation

F1 Pick up 10 beads, run through all the beads again and the next two or three beads once more, taking care not to split the thread. Do not knot.

F2 (Pick up 2, miss 1, go through 1) 5 times. Step up through the first two beads added in the round.

Petals

1 Stitch 2 beads on to each bead of the pair of beads added in the Foundation (4 beads in the row).

2 Increase by 1 bead at each end of the row (6 beads).

3 Increase by 1 bead at each end of the row (8 beads).

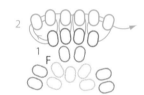

4 Work straight.

5 Decrease by 1 bead at each edge (6 beads).

6 Decrease by 1 bead at each edge (4 beads)

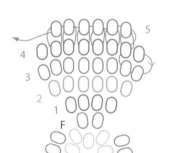

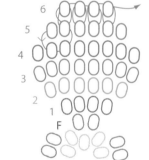

7 Weave back down to the bottom of the petal, going backwards and forwards across the rows. Pulling the thread firmly as you go will help the petal curve gently into a cupped shape (a softer tension will produce a less pronounced curve). Once you have gone through the Foundation Row of 2 beads, go through the next bead on the inner circle of beads and through the next pair of beads added in the Foundation.

Make four more petals by repeating Steps 1 – 7.

Variation 1

Foundation
Work as *Basic Square Stitch Flower*

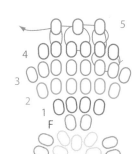

Petals

1 – 3 Work as *Basic Square Stitch Flower* (4, 6 & 8 beads).

4 Decrease by 1 bead at the beginning of the row by going through the bead on the edge of the 2nd Row, turn and go through the second to last bead of the 3rd Row. Decrease by 1 bead at the end of the row (6 beads).

5 Decrease by 1 bead on each edge and by 1 bead in the centre of the row (3 beads).

6 Pick up 1 bead and go through the bead on the end of the previous row (4th), towards the outside of the petal. Pick up 2 beads and go through the end bead of the next row down (3rd). Go through the next row down (2nd) to the other side of the petal. Go through the end bead of the row above (3rd) pointing towards the centre of the petal. Pick up 2 beads and go up through the end bead of the next row up (4th); pick up 1 bead and go through the top row.

7 Weave down as Step 7 of *Basic Square Stitch Flower*. Make four more petals.

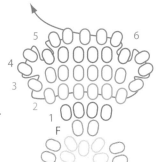

◆◆◆

Variation 2

Foundation
Work as *Basic Square Stitch Flower*

Petals

1 & 2 Work as *Basic Square Stitch Flower* (4 & 6 beads).

3 & 4 Work straight.

5 Decrease by 1 bead on each edge (4 beads).

6 Work straight.

7 Decrease by 1 bead on each edge (2 beads).

8a Go through the 2 beads in the centre of Row 6 and up through the bead on the edge of Row 7, pointing towards the centre of the petal. Pick up 1 bead, go through the next bead and down through the bead on the edge of Row 6 and across through Row 5.

8b Pick up 1 bead and go down through the bead on the edge of Row 4, across through Row 3 and up through the bead on the edge of Row 4. Pick up 1 bead, go through Row 5.

9 Weave down as Step 7 of *Basic Square Stitch Flower*. Make four more petals.

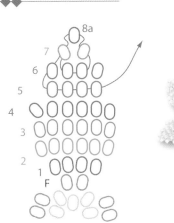

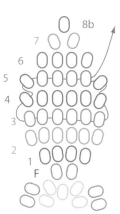

Variation 3

Foundation

Pick up 10 beads, run through all the beads again and the next two or three beads once more, taking care not to split the thread. Do not knot.

(Pick up 3, miss 1, go through 1) 5 times. Step up through the first three beads added in the round.

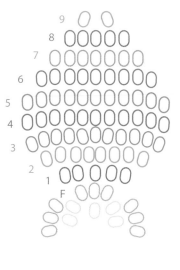

Petals

1 Increase by 1 bead at each end of the row (5 beads).

2 & 3 Increase by 1 bead at each edge and in the centre of the row (8 & 11 beads).

4 & 5 Work straight.

6, 7 & 8 Decrease by 1 bead on each edge of each row. (9, 7 & 5 beads)

9 Stitch 1 bead on to each of the 2nd and 4th beads of the 8th Row. Go through the 3 beads in the centre of the 8th Row once more and the beads of the 9th Row to pull them closely together (2 beads).

10 Weave down through the lower rows to the base of the petal. Reinforce the stitching of the 3 beads of the Foundation to the inner ring of beads (it will very likely be wobbly by now) before continuing around the ring to the next group of 3 beads of the Foundation.

Make four more petals.

◆◆◆

Variation 4

Foundation
Work as *Variation 3*.

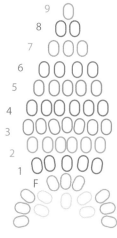

Petals

1 Increase by 1 bead at each end of the row (5 beads).

2 & 3 Increase by 1 bead in the centre of the row (6 & 7 beads).

4 – 9 Decrease by 1 bead in the centre of each row, concluding with 1 bead at the tip of the petal.

10 As Step 10 of *Variation 3*.

Make four more petals.

Tip
If you wish to produce a more gradual bend in the petal, add one or two straight rows in between Rows 3 and 4.

Variation 5

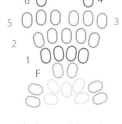

Foundation
Work as *Basic Square Stitch Flower*

Petals

1 Work as *Basic Square Stitch Flower* (4 beads).

2 Increase by 1 in the centre of the row (5 beads).

3 Stitch 1 bead on to the 1st bead and 2 beads on to the next bead. Turn.

4a Working on the right hand side of the petal, decrease by 1 bead on the edge. Stitch 1 bead on to the centre bead of Row 3.

4b Go through the centre bead of Row 3 once more. Continuing in the same direction, go through the next bead, the centre bead of the row below (2nd Row) and the 2 beads to the left of it to exit the edge of the petal.

5 & 6 As Steps 3 & 4 on the left hand side of the petal.

7 Weave down as Step 7 of *Basic Square Stitch Flower*. Make four more petals.

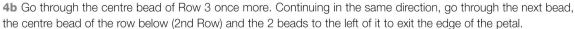

Variation 6

Foundation
Work as *Basic Square Stitch Flower*

Petals

1 Stitch 1 bead on to each bead of the foundation pair (2 beads).

2 – 4 Work straight.

5 Stitch 1 bead on to the 2 beads of the row below. Weave down to the base of the petal and go through the next bead on the inner circle.

6 Stitch 2 beads on to the single bead of the inner circle.

7 – 10 Work straight.

11 Work as Row 5 then weave down to the base of the petal and go through the next pair of beads added in the Foundation.

Repeat from Step 1 four times to make 10 petals in all.

Variation 7

Foundation
Work as *Basic Square Stitch Flower*

Petals

1 & 2 Increase by 1 bead in the centre of the row (3 & 4 beads).

3 Increase by 1 bead at each end of the row (6 beads).

4 Increase by 1 bead on each of the 3rd and 4th beads (8 beads).

5 Work straight.

6 & 7 Decrease by 1 bead on each edge (6 & 4 beads).

8 Weave down as Step 7 of the *Basic Square Stitch Flower*.

Make four more petals.

Water Lily SQUARE STITCH

Tantalisingly viewed from the pond's edge, this tranquil yet dazzling flower lights up its surroundings like a delicate jewel. In our beaded version there are three layers, so you need to make the Foundation carefully and keep working steadily outwards.

FIDDLY FACTOR

SHOPPING LIST

seed beads (any size 10 -15) or cylinders

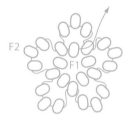

F1 Pick up 10 beads, run through all the beads again and the next two or three beads once more, taking care not to split the thread. Do not knot.

F2 (Pick up 3, miss 1, go through 1) 5 times. Go through the next bead on the inner circle.

F3 (Pick up 2, miss 1 bead on the inner circle, go through the next) 5 times.
Go through the first 2 beads added in the round

The groups of 3 beads will form the base of the middle petals of the flower and the pairs of beads will form the base of the inner petals. Start by working on the inner petals.

Inner Petals

1 Increase by 1 bead on each edge (4 beads)

2 & 3 Increase by 1 bead in the centre of the row (5 & 6 beads)

4, 5, 6 & 7 Decrease by 1 bead in the centre of the row (5, 4, 3 & 2 beads)

Weave down as described in Step 7 of the *Basic Square Stitch Flower*.

Make four more inner petals.
Go through the next bead of the inner circle and the first group of 3 beads of the Foundation.

Middle Petals

1 Work straight (3 beads).

2 & 3 Increase by 1 bead on each edge (5 & 7 beads).

4 Work straight.

5 Decrease by 1 on each edge (5 beads).

6 Work straight.

7 Decrease by 1 on each edge (3 beads).

8 Decrease by 1 in the centre (2 beads).

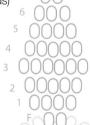

Outer Petals

Foundation

Pick up 3 beads and go through the centre bead of the Foundation beads at the base of the next Middle Petal. Continue around placing 3 beads in between each of the Middle Petals. Work off each new set of 3 beads in turn to make the Outer Petals.

The Petals

1 - 6 Work as for the Middle Petal.

7 Work straight.

8 Decrease by 1 bead on each edge (3 beads)

9 Work straight.

10 Decrease by 1 in the centre (2 beads).

11 Add beads around the edges of the petal as for the Middle Petal, but this time placing the beads in the upper position between Rows 8 & 7. Weave back and forth across the petal to get to the correct positions.

12 Weave to the base of the petal, adding an extra bead on top of Row 2 as in Step 10 of the Middle Petal.

Go through the next group of 3 beads added in the Outer Petal Foundation.

Make four more Outer Petals.

Stamens

You might find it useful to stitch one or two beads across the centre of the inner ring of beads of the Foundation before adding the stamens, which are 3 to 6 beads long *(see page 89)*.

9 Go down through Row 7, pick up 1, go through the bead on the edge of Row 6, pick up 2 and go through the bead on the edge of Row 4. Go across Row 3 and up through the bead on the edge of Row 4. Pick up 2 and go up through the bead on the edge of Row 6; pick up 1 and go up through Row 7 and the bead on the edge of Row 8. Pick up 1 and go down through the other bead of Row 8.

10 Weave down through the edge beads and the lower rows towards the base of the petal. Working on the inside surface of the petal, at Row 2, go through the edge bead, pick up 1 and go through the bead on the other end of the row, pulling the thread very tightly so that the petal is pulled in at the sides. Continue weaving down and go through the next group of 3 beads added in the Foundation.

Make four more Middle Petals. At the bottom of the final Middle Petal, only go through 2 of the beads in the next group of Foundation beads.

Trellis Bracelet

SHOPPING LIST

10g seed bead size 11 in a mix of shades of blue and purple (S)

10g 6mm twisted bugles (B)

32 x 3mm Swarovski bicone crystals

toggle clasp (optional)

1 Water Lily made using cylinders with size 15 seed beads
for the stamens

The twisted bugle beads we have used in the base of this bracelet twinkle like the reflections in a pond. Each block of bugles is linked to the next by little daisy motifs in a mix of watery shades and we have added some rippling netting along the edges at the centre of the bracelet to highlight the lovely water lily.

Start by making the first *Bugle Block* and a set of linking daisies, then add a *Standard Bugle Block*. Continue alternating linking daisies and *Standard Bugle Blocks* until the bracelet is the length you require, allowing for one final block and the fastening. Add the final *Bugle Block*, which mirrors the first, and the embellishment. Finally, make the toggle and loop fastening or, if you prefer, use a purchased one.

First Bugle Block

1 Pick up 9S, 1B,1S. Go back through 8S and pull through so that the 8S are sitting alongside 1S, 1B, 1S and then go through those 3 beads. *Pick up 1S, 1B, 1S (a bugle set) and go through the previous set and the new set once more. Repeat from * once.

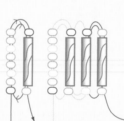

2 Fold the strip of beadwork back on itself and go through the 8S and the last bugle set once more so they are joined firmly together. Go through the 3rd set added.

Linking daisies

* Pick up 4S and go back through the bead the thread is coming from. Pick up 2S and go through the 3rd bead just added.
** Pass through the next 2S and the bugle set below.
Repeat from * – **. Pass through the next 2S, go across through the bead at the centre of the 'daisy' and through the next bead pointing towards the 1st daisy.

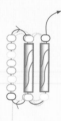

Standard Bugle Block

1 Pick up 1B and link to the opposite daisy by going through the 2nd of the 2S picked up when making it. The bugle and the S either side of it form the 1st bugle set of this block.

2 * Pick up 1 bugle set and go through the previous set and the new set once more. Repeat from * twice. Fold the strip of beadwork back on itself and go through the 1st and last bugle sets once more so they are joined firmly together. Go through the 3rd set added.

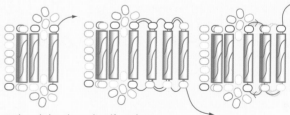

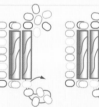

Final Bugle Block

Make as a *Standard Block* but substitute 8S for the 3rd bugle set. Weave through the beads of this block several times to strengthen it, particularly the 8S. Finish by passing through 5 of the 8S. Do not finish off the thread as you will return to it later for the fastening.

Embellishment

1 With the thread exiting the middle bead at the top of the 3rd daisy from the central block of the bracelet, * pick up 5S and go through the middle bead at the top of the next daisy. Repeat from * 4 times.

2 Turn by hooking around the thread between the beads and go back through the last 3 beads added. * Pick up 1S, 1crystal, 1S, 1crystal, 1S and go through the same middle bead of the next daisy. Repeat from * 3 times.

3 Turn again and repeat Row 2, going through the same beads as before.

4 Turn and pass through the last set of beads added and the middle bead. Pick up 7S and go through the next middle bead, placing the new beads between the two crystal groups. Repeat from * once.

Repeat Steps 1 – 4 on the other side of the bracelet.

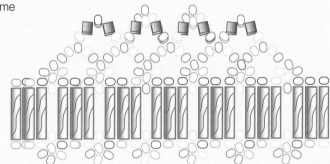

centre block

Finally, stitch the Water Lily in place, anchoring it securely by going through the 3 Foundation beads at the base of each outer Petal.

Toggle and Loop Fastening

The Toggle

1 Make a *Bugle Block* as for the first block of the bracelet. Weave through the beads of this block several times to strengthen it, particularly the 8S. Finish by passing through 5 of the 8S.

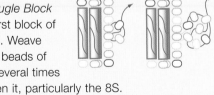

2 Pick up 1S, turn and go back through the bead next to the one the thread is coming from. Pick up 1S and go back through the last bead added.

3 Pick up 3S and go through the bead next to the one the thread is coming from. Pick up 2S and go through the 2nd bead just added.

4 To connect the toggle to the bracelet, pass through the 4th bead of the 8S of the first block of the bracelet, pointing towards the 5th bead. Go through the next bead on the edge of the daisy and back into the 5th bead of the 8S. Weave through the connecting beads a few times and finish off the thread.

The Loop

Return to the thread left at the final block of the bracelet to make the loop.

Repeat Steps 2 and 3 of the toggle to make a line of 'Daisies in a Row' (like the braid on *page 100*) which will form a loop long enough to accommodate the toggle (ours was 5 daisies long). Stitch the 2 beads on the edge of the last daisy securely to the 2 beads in the centre of the 8S and finish off the thread.

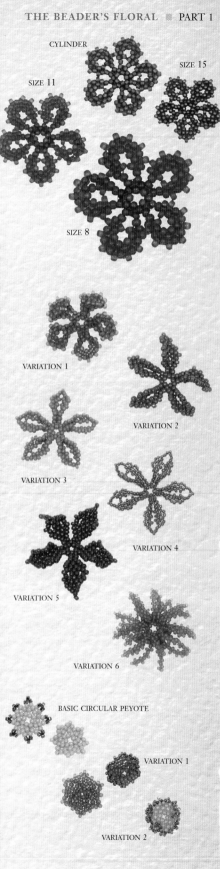

CYLINDER

SIZE 15

SIZE 11

SIZE 8

VARIATION 1

VARIATION 2

VARIATION 3

VARIATION 4

VARIATION 5

VARIATION 6

BASIC CIRCULAR PEYOTE

VARIATION 1

VARIATION 2

Peyote Stitch Filigree Flowers

These frothy open weave flowers are light and airy and suit being gathered together en masse, as though in a herbacious border. The shapes call to mind arum lilies, clematis and poinsettias while the final many-petalled variation could be a Michaelmas daisy or marguerite.

General notes

■ Once you have made the two base rows each petal is worked separately. Before you start, remember to look at the *Tips and Techniques Section* on *pages 8 & 9*.

Basic Peyote Stitch Flower

Foundation

F1 Pick up 10 beads, run through all the beads again and the next two or three beads once more, taking care not to split the thread. Do not knot.

F2 (Pick up 2, miss 1, go through 1) 5 times. Step up through the first bead added in the round (Bead A).

Petal

1 Pick up 11 beads and go down through the 2nd bead added in the previous round (Bead B).

2 Go up through Bead A and the next bead. As you do this, Beads A and B will twist so that they sit horizontally side by side at the base of the petal. Pick up 1, miss 1, go through 1. (Pick up 2, miss 1, go through 1) 3 times. Pick up 1, miss 1, go through 1 and Bead B.

3 Go up through bead A, through the next bead and the 1st bead added on the last round. (Pick up 1, go through 1) 7 times. Go through the next bead and down through Bead B.

For each of the next four petals:
Pass through the next bead of the inner circle and up through the 1st bead of the next pair added in the Foundation. Work each petal the same as the first, reading Beads A & B to mean the pair of beads added in the Foundation. Having completed the final petal, secure both ends of thread.

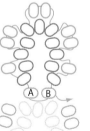

Variation 1

Foundation

Work as *Basic Peyote Stitch Flower*.

Petal

1 Work as *Basic Peyote Stitch Flower*.

2 Go through Bead A and the next bead. (Pick up 2, miss 1, go through 1) 5 times. Go down through Bead B.

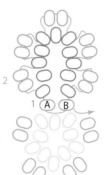

3 Go up through Bead A, the next bead and the 1st bead of the 1st pair added in Step 2.
(Pick up 1, go through 1) 9 times. Go through the next bead and down through Bead B.

Work four more petals, travelling from one to the next as described in *Basic Peyote Stitch Flower*.

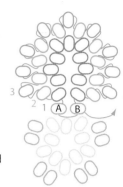

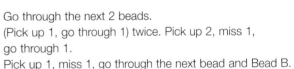

Variation 2

You will find that the petals of this variation will curl and twist at their will, not yours! You might find this disconcerting if you are looking for something flat and symmetrical. But it means that you can create naturalistic arrangements of flowers very easily by combining several of these together.

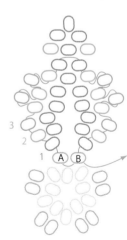

Foundation

Work as *Basic Peyote Stitch Flower*.

Petal

1 Pick up 11 beads. Go back through the 4th bead from the needle and pull up tight. Pick up 1, miss 1 and go through the next bead. Pick up 5 and go down through the 2nd bead added in the previous round (Bead B).

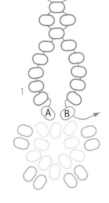

2 Go through Bead A and the next bead.
Pick up 1, miss 1, go through 1.
Pick up 2, miss 1, go through 1.
(Pick up 1, go through 1) twice.

Go through the next 2 beads.
(Pick up 1, go through 1) twice. Pick up 2, miss 1, go through 1.
Pick up 1, miss 1, go through the next bead and Bead B.

3 Go up Bead A, the next bead and the 1st bead added on the last round.
(Pick up 1, go through 1) 3 times.
Go up through the next bead, turn and go down through the adjacent bead and the next bead.
(Pick up 1, go through 1) 3 times.
Go through the next bead and Bead B.

Work four more petals, travelling from one to the next as described in *Basic Peyote Stitch Flower*.

Variation 3

Foundation

Work as *Basic Peyote Stitch Flower*.

Petal

1 Pick up 18 beads and go down through the 2nd bead added in the previous round (Bead B).

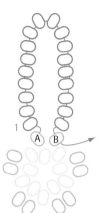

2 Go up through Bead A. (Pick up 1, miss 1, go through 1) 4 times. Go through the next bead. Pick up 1, go through 2. (Pick up 1, miss 1, go through 1) 4 times.

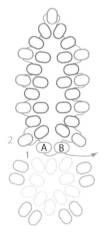

3a Go up through Bead A and the bead immediately above it (Bead C, ie the first of the 18 beads picked up in Step 1). Go down through the bead to the right (Bead D, ie the last of the 18 beads picked up in Step 1) and Bead B. Pull up tight so that Beads C and D sit side by side.

3b Go up through Bead A and the 1st bead picked up in Step 2.
* Pick up 1, go through 1. Pick up 2, go through 1. Pick up 1, go through 1.** Go through 6 beads, working around the outside edge of the petal.
Repeat from * to **.

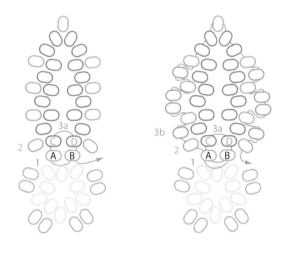

4 *(Not illustrated)* Fold the petal at the base to bring the outside edges close to each other. Stitch the two bottom beads (ie the first and last beads added in Step 2) firmly together. Go through Bead B.

Work four more petals, travelling from one to the next as described in *Basic Peyote Stitch Flower*.

> ## *Tip*
> When working Step 4, hold the petal between finger and thumb so that the two sides of the petal are flat against each other. Open the petal up again once the stitching is completed.

Variation 4

This is a larger version of Variation 3

Foundation

Work as *Basic Peyote Stitch Flower*.

Petal

1 Pick up 24 beads and go down through the 2nd bead added in the previous round (Bead B).

2 Go up through Bead A. (Pick up 1, miss 1, go through 1) 5 times.
Go through 2 beads. Pick up 1, go through 3.
(Pick up 1, miss 1, go through 1) 5 times.

3a Go up through Bead A and the bead immediately above it (Bead C, ie the first of the 24 beads picked up in Step 1). Go down through the bead to the right (Bead D, ie the last of the 24 beads picked up in step 1) and Bead B. Pull up tight so that Beads C and D sit side by side.

3b Go up through Bead A and the 1st bead picked up in Step 2.
(Pick up 1, go through 1) twice. Pick up 2, go through 1.
Pick up 1, go through 1.
Go through 8 beads, working around the outside edge of the petal.
Pick up 1, go through 1. Pick up 2, go through 1.
(Pick up 1, go through 1) twice.

4 Turn and go up through Bead D and the next 2 beads above it on the inside of the petal.
(Pick up 1, go through 1) three times.
Go through the next 8 beads on the inside edge of the petal.
(Pick up 1, go through 1) three times.
Weave down to and through Bead C and then out through the bead at the bottom of the outside edge of the petal.

5 *(Not illustrated)* Fold the petal at the base to bring the outside edges close to each other. Stitch the two bottom beads (ie the first and last beads added in Step 2) firmly together.
Go through Bead B.

Work four more petals, travelling from one to the next as described in *Basic Peyote Stitch Flower*.

Variation 5

Make sure you pull the thread up really tight in Steps 3 & 4 of this variation to achieve the shape of the petal. Don't be nervous about it – you need to hear the beads 'click' into place. If you turn this flower over and press down in the centre, you get a completely different look.

Foundation

Work as *Basic Peyote Stitch Flower*.

Petal

1 Pick up 11, miss 1 bead and go back down through the next bead.
(Pick up 1, miss 1, go through 1) 5 times (The last bead you go through is Bead B.)

2 Go up through Bead A and the bead immediately above it. (Pick up 1, go through 1) 4 times. Turn and go down through the adjacent bead. (Pick up 1, go through 1) 4 times.

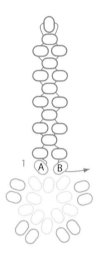

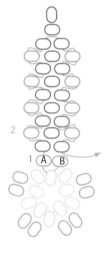

3 Go up through the adjacent bead and the bead above it, keeping to the outer edge of the petal.
Pick up 1, go through 1.
(Pick up 2, go through 1) twice.
Go through the next bead, turn and go back down through the adjacent bead and the next bead.
(Pick up 2, go through 1) twice.
Pick up 1, go through 1.
Go through the next bead.

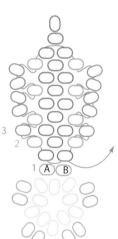

4 Turn and go up through the adjacent bead and 2 more beads on the outside edge of the petal.
(Pick up 1, go through 1) 3 times, placing the 2nd bead in between the first pair of beads added in Step 3.
Go through the next 3 beads, turn and go down through the adjacent bead and the next 3 beads on the outside edge of the petal.
(Pick up 1, go through 1) 3 times.
Encourage the petal to bend over backwards at the tip.
Go down through the next 2 beads and Bead B.

Work four more petals, travelling from one to the next as described in *Basic Peyote Stitch Flower*.

Variation 6

This variation makes a very simple but effective daisy shape. Some of the petals will curve gently, rather than being perfectly straight as shown in the diagrams. This is due to the inevitable unevenness of the beads – however slight – and adds to the naturalness and charm of the flower. Experiment with different colour combinations and lengths of petal – you will discover a whole world of daisy-shaped flowers once you start to look out for them!

Foundation

As *Basic Peyote Stitch Flower.*

Petal

1 * Pick up 12 beads. Go back through the 4th bead from the needle and pull up tight. (Pick up 1, miss 1, go through 1) 4 times. ** Go down through Bead A.

2 Go up through Bead B. Repeat from * to **. Go down through Bead B.

3 Repeat from * to **. Go up through the next Bead A.

Repeat Steps 1, 2 & 3 around the Foundation (15 petals in all).

4 Now weave down to the inner circle and bring the needle up between any two of the circle beads. Make a petal as before but starting with 10 beads and go through the next circle bead. The new petal should lie in front of the ones already made. Repeat around the circle of beads until you have made ten of these shorter petals.

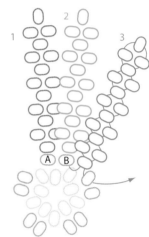

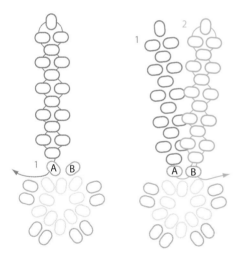

Tip

Support each new petal over your index finger as you work, holding the petals already made out of the way with your other fingers and thumb. This will help to avoid your thread catching on to the other petals, which can be very irritating as well as harmful to the thread.

*The following flowers are worked in Circular Peyote Stitch so, rather
than working separate petals, all the petals are made at the same time,
building row upon row. They are identical in the centre but each one has
a different edging.*

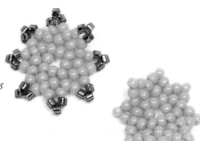

Basic Circular Peyote Stitch Flower

Foundation

F1 Pick up 8 beads, run through all the beads again and the next two or three
beads once more, taking care not to split the thread. Do not knot.

F2 (Pick up 2, miss 1, go through 1) 4 times. Go through the first bead
added in the round (Bead A). This is the 'step up' at the end of the round.

1 (Pick up 1, go through 1) 8 times. Step up at the end of the round.

2 (Pick up 2, go through 1) 8 times. Step up at the end of the round.

3 * Pick up 1 bead (or 3 smaller beads) and
go through the next bead. Take the needle
down through the next bead of the previous
round and up the next bead to the outside
edge. Repeat from * 7 times.

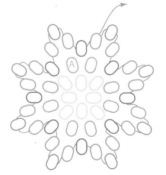

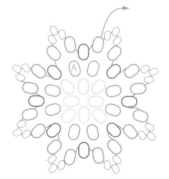

Variation 1

Foundation & 1 Work as F1, F2 & 1 of *Basic Circular Peyote Stitch Flower*

2 (Pick up 1, go through 1; pick up 2, go through 1) 4 times. Step up at the end of the round.

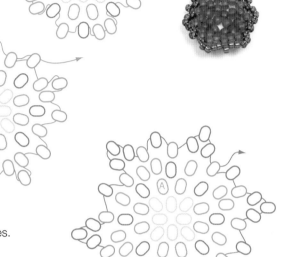

3 (Pick up 1, go through 1) 12 times. Step up at the end of the round.

4 (Pick up 1, go through 1; pick up 3, go through 1) 6 times.

Note: If you work rounds 3 & 4 in smaller beads, the flower is pulled up into a little cup shape.

◆◆◆

Variation 2

Foundation, 1 & 2 Work as F1, F2, 1 & 2 of *Basic Circular Peyote Stitch Flower*

3 Stitch 3 smaller beads between EVERY bead of the last round. Do NOT step up at the end of the round.

4 Repeat the 3rd round, stitching through the same beads as before.

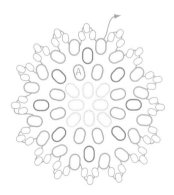

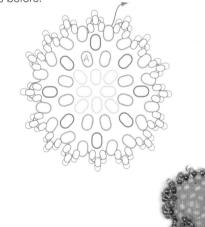

Clematis PEYOTE STITCH

There can be few sights more typical of an English country garden than the massed blooms of a clematis rambling over a wall or pergola. These little flowers are quick to make once you get in the swing, so make lots of them in several shades of the same colour to get the full showy effect.

Foundation
Use all C beads

F1 Pick up 6 beads, run through all the beads again and the next two or three beads once more, taking care not to split the thread. Do not knot.

F2 (Pick up 2, miss 1, go through 1) 3 times.

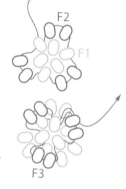

F3 Go through the next bead on the inner circle. (Pick up 2, miss 1 bead on the inner circle, go through the next bead) 3 times. Go through the first bead added in the round (Bead A).

The pairs of beads added in F2 will form the base of the lower petals of the flower and the pairs of beads added in F3 will form the base of the upper petals.

Petals
Start by working the three upper petals. Then weave down to the lower level of the Foundation to work the three lower petals – you might find it easiest to turn the flower over so that you are looking at it from the back.

FIDDLY FACTOR
❀❀ ❀❀

SHOPPING LIST

cylinders or seed beads
(any size 10 -15)
in two shades:
for the centre (C) and
for the edges of
the petals (E)

Each petal is worked as *Peyote Stitch Flower, Variation 2*. We have placed beads of one shade along the centre of each petal and surrounded them with edge beads of a different shade. The instructions below tell you the order to pick up the differently shaded beads and the diagram of the petal shows the final positions of the two shades. For the step by step diagrams, refer back to *Variation 2* of the *Peyote Stitch Filigree Flower* on *page 39*

1 Pick up 6C and 5E. Go back through the 4th bead from the needle and pull up tight. Pick up 1E, miss 1 and go through the next bead. Pick up 5C and go down through the 2nd bead added in the previous round (Bead B).

2 Use all E beads and work as Row 2 of *Variation 2, Peyote Stitch Filigree Flower*.

3 Use all E beads and work as Row 3 of *Variation 2, Peyote Stitch Filigree Flower*.

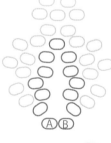

Finally, with the front of the flower facing you, make sure that each petal is 'folded' in the centre with its edges upwards and the tip of the petal pointing downwards.
You will find that the flower is slightly raised in the centre – press down on it as you attach the flower to your chosen background through the central hole of the flower, adding the stamens as you do so.

Garland Pin

FIDDLY FACTOR

Cover the lower bar of the kilt pin with foliage

1 Tie your thread to the unopening side of the kilt pin. * Pick up 3G, let them drop down to the kilt pin and hold them gently against it while you pass the needle around the wire and down through the third bead (be careful to go into the bead from the same side as the thread is exiting.) When you pull the thread through, the beads will settle up against the kilt pin with one bead making a 'picot' in between the other two.

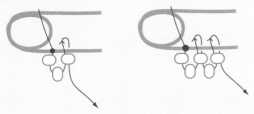

2 Repeat from * but this time picking up only 2G and going through the second of them.

3 Repeat Step 2 across the kilt pin, pushing the beads as closely together on the wire as they will go, until the end is reached. (We counted 25 picot beads on our pin.)

4 Turn by looping around the thread and stitching back through the last picot bead. * Pick up 3S and go through the next picot bead. Repeat from * all across the row. The beads will be very tightly packed and so will 'ruffle'. Arrange them so that all the threads are on one side of the wire, at the back of the brooch, with the beadwork at the front.

5 Refer to the instructions on *pages 90 & 91* for making greenery. Use the green beads of both sizes to make a few leaves. Work back through the beads of the last row, adding in some tendrils as you go and stitching the leaves in place evenly across the width of the kilt pin.

Add flowers

1 Attach one of the larger clematis to the kilt pin: with thread exiting the top of one of the G beads of the 1st Row, * pass through the centre of the clematis, a 4 mm bicone crystal and 1S. Go back through the crystal, the clematis and the G bead. Turn by looping around the kilt pin and go back up through the G bead, then repeat from * to strengthen and reinforce the stitching. Secure the thread into the beadwork.

2 Attach a new thread to the kilt pin at one end of it. * Pick up (1F, 1 x 3 mm crystal) 3 times **, 1F and 1 x 4 mm round crystal. Repeat from * 7 times and from * – ** once more to form a long 'swag' from one end of the kilt pin to the other. Attach securely to the kilt pin. Return through the last few beads added and stitch a large clematis to one of the F beads near the top of the swag as described in Step 1 (turn by stitching into the F from the opposite side).

3 Make a shorter 'swag' inside the first: pick up (1L, 1 x 4 mm crystal) 18 times and one more L and attach to the kilt pin. Stitch on the smaller clematis as before using a smaller crystal.

4 Finally, sew a few pressed glass flower beads in among the foliage.

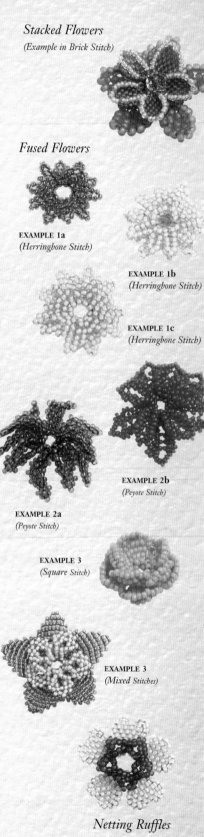

Stacked Flowers
(Example in Brick Stitch)

Fused Flowers

EXAMPLE 1a
(Herringbone Stitch)

EXAMPLE 1b
(Herringbone Stitch)

EXAMPLE 1c
(Herringbone Stitch)

EXAMPLE 2b
(Peyote Stitch)

EXAMPLE 2a
(Peyote Stitch)

EXAMPLE 3
(Square Stitch)

EXAMPLE 3
(Mixed Stitches)

Netting Ruffles

Double Flowers

All of the Basic Flowers and Variations we have shown you in the preceding pages can be made into Double Flowers. You could also combine petals of two variations or even different stitches to benefit from the particular nature of each. There are so many possible permutations that we have not attempted a 'Basic with Variations' for each of the three methods of making Double Flowers presented here. Instead, we have made examples for you in a selection of stitches to illustrate the general points – you will find many more.

Stacked Flowers

The simplest way of creating a *Double Flower* is to make two flowers and then stack one on top of the other, stitching them together as you add the stamens. This is particularly helpful if you make a mistake in one of the flowers – adding another flower on top will hide where you went wrong!

Example: using *Brick Stitch Blossom Flowers*

Variation 2 of the *Brick Stitch Blossom Flowers* made in size 15 seed beads (note how pretty it is if you use a lighter shade for the outside edges of the petals) nestles on top of a *Basic Brick Stitch Blossom Flower* made in size 8 seed beads. The two flowers were made separately and sewn together when adding the crystal 'stamen'.

Fused Flowers

A *Double Flower* can also be created by making a flower and then working a second complete flower layer on to the original Foundation Row. In some instances you may need to use a finer needle for the initial row of the second layer. Here are diagrams to show you how to arrange the beads at the centre so that the two layers sit staggered against each other. On the next page are some examples to get you started.

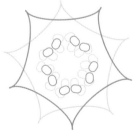

This is the arrangement of beads at the centre if the base layer is a *Herringbone Stitch Daisy Flower* or a *Brick Stitch Blossom Flower*.

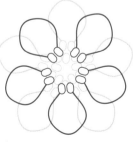

This is the arrangement of beads at the centre if the base layer is a *Square Stitch Cupped Flower* or a *Peyote Stitch Filigree Flower*.

Example 1 : using *Herringbone Daisy Flowers*

1a *Two layers of Variation 1*

1b *Two layers of Variation 2*

1c *Two layers of Variation 3*

Example 2 : using *Peyote Stitch Filigree Flowers*

2a *Two layers of Variation 2*

2b *Variation 3 worked on top of Variation 4*

Example 3: using *Square Stitch Cupped Flowers*

Two layers of Variation 1

Example 4: mixing stitches

Variation 4 of the Square Stitch Cupped Flowers combined with Variation 1 of the Peyote Stitch Filigree Flowers (at the front).

Netting Ruffles

Alternatively, instead of working a complete second layer on a flower, you can add just a suggestion of one in a simple frilly layer of *Netting Ruffles*.

First, make a flower from any in the *Stitch Primer*. Do not finish off the working thread.

Next, add a *Netting Ruffle*:

1 Weave back to the Foundation Row and * pick up 3 beads and pass through the next 2 beads in the Foundation Row. Repeat from * around the circle. Pass the needle up through the centre bead of the first group of 3 just added.

2 Pick up 7 beads and pass the needle through the middle bead of the next set of 3. Continue around, and then pass through the same middle bead as in the previous row.

3 Pick up 5 beads and pass through the next centre bead as in the previous row, keeping this set of 5 in front of the set of 7. Continue around.

4 Pick up 3 beads and work in the same manner all the way around.

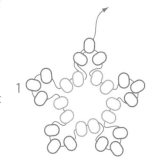

A Netting Ruffle worked on Variation 4 of the Brick Stitch Blossom Flowers

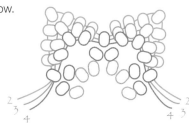

49

Basic Herringbone Tubular Flowers

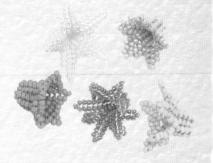

Tubular Herringbone Flowers

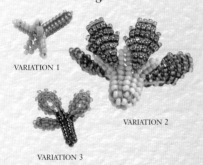

VARIATION 1

VARIATION 2

VARIATION 3

Basic Peyote Stitch Tubular Flowers

VARIATION 1

VARIATION 2

Flowers with tubes added

An example of a Herringbone tube

EXAMPLE 1
Using Peyote tubes

EXAMPLE 2
Using Peyote tubes

Tubular Flowers

All of the Basic Flowers and Variations can also be made into Tubular Flowers using either of two methods. We have called the first method 'Tube first, then Flower'. You start with a section of tubular beadwork and then, when it is the length you require, add any of the Basic Flowers or their Variations. Alternatively, you can make your chosen flower and then return to the Foundation Row and add some tubular beadwork at the back of the flower. We have called this second method 'Flower first, then Tube'.

Herringbone and Peyote Stitches are the best to use for Tubular flowers, and they work equally well for both methods of construction.

Tube first, then flower – using *Herringbone Tubes*

Basic Herringbone Tubular Flower

The following instructions for the *Basic Herringbone Tubular Flower* give you a tube with five ribs around *(see top left)*. But you can make a narrower or wider tube by starting with fewer or more beads, as long as it is an even number. The smallest tube you can make starts with a foundation of just 4 beads to give two ribs.

F & 1 The foundation and first row are worked the same as F & 1 of the *Basic Herringbone Daisy Flower* on *page 12.*

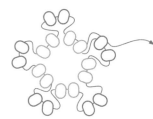

2 * Pick up 2 and pass down into the bead below and up the adjacent bead. Continue around, repeating from *. Step up at the end of the row.

To make the work easier to handle, place it on to a cocktail stick or cotton wool bud (or any suitable form of the correct size), and pull the thread gently whilst pressing the beads into a tubular shape.

3 Repeat Row 2 until the tube is the length you want. In the case of our examples, this was two or three times.

4 Now make a flower directly on top of the *Herringbone* tube, using each pair of beads at the top of the tube as though it were a pair of beads of the Foundation of your chosen flower. We have chosen *Herringbone Daisy Flower Variations* for our illustration at top left.

Tip

If you choose to make the petals using *Variations 3* or *4* of the *Square Stitch Cupped Flowers*, you will need to add an extra bead in the centre of each pair of beads at the top of the *Herringbone* tube so that you have a foundation for each petal of 3 beads.

Variation 1

F, 1 & 2 As for *Basic Herringbone Tubular Flower*, but starting with 4 beads in the Foundation circle.

Repeat Row 2 six times.

Change bead colour and work *Variation 2* of the *Herringbone Daisy Flowers*.

◆◆◆

Variation 2

F, 1 & 2 As for *Basic Herringbone Tubular Flower*, but starting with 12 beads in the Foundation circle.

3, 4 & 5 Work as Row 2.

6 Place 2 beads on to each rib and 1 bead in a different shade (D) between each rib.

7 Place 2 beads on to each rib and 2 beads in D between each rib.

8 Place 3 beads on to each rib, passing through the 2 beads between the ribs without adding any beads.

9 Using D beads, work *Square Stitch Flower, Variation 7* (omitting Row 5) on each pair of beads between the ribs.

10 Reduce the circle at the beginning of the tube – *see Tip, right*.

Tip

If you wish to neaten the base of a wide tube, put a needle on the tail of thread at the start of the tube. *Square Stitch* 1 bead on to each of the pairs of beads picked up for the Foundation, then run through them all again to pull them together into a smaller circle.

Variation 3

◆◆◆

F, 1 & 2 As for *Basic Herringbone Tubular Flower*, but starting with 4 beads in the Foundation circle.

3, 4, 5 & 6 Work as Row 2.

7 & 8 Work as Rows 2 and 3 of *Herringbone Flower Variation 2 (page 13)* to give four pairs of beads at the top of the tube.

Finally, work a *Basic Peyote Stitch* petal *(page 38)* on each pair of beads.

Tube first, then flower – using *Peyote Tubes*

Basic Peyote Stitch Tubular Flower

F1 The first row of the Foundation is worked the same as F1 of the *Basic Peyote Stitch Filigree Flower* on *page 38*.

F2 (Pick up 1, miss 1, go through 1) 5 times. Step up through the first bead added in the round.

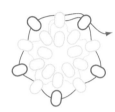

1 (Pick up 1, go through the next bead added in the last round) 5 times. Step up through the first bead added in the round.

2 Repeat Row 1 until the tube is the length you want, adding 5 beads each time you go around and stepping up at the end of the round.

3 Final Row. You must work one increase row before making any petals: (pick up 2, go through the next bead added in the last round) 5 times. Step up.

4 Now make a flower directly on top of the *Peyote* tube, using each pair of beads added in the final row at the top of the tube as though it were a pair of beads of the Foundation of your chosen flower. We have used the *Basic Brick Stitch Blossom Flower* for our illustration.

> ### *Tip*
> The petals of *Variations 3 & 4* of the *Square Stitch Flowers* need 3 beads in their Foundation, so work the increase round picking up 3 rather than 2 beads.

Peyote Stitch Tubular Flower Variations

The instructions for the *Basic Peyote Stitch Tubular Flower* give you a tube with 5 pairs of beads at the top of it from which to work your petals. But you can make a narrower or wider tube by starting with fewer or more beads, though it must always be an even number. We find that the smallest tube that works satisfactorily in *Peyote Stitch* starts with 8 beads in the Foundation circle – any narrower and the tube becomes very floppy with too much thread showing.

> ### *Tip*
> To neaten the base of a wide tube, run through the beads which sit right at the centre of the circle at the start of the tube (they are the ones which were missed in F2 of the Foundation) and pull them together tightly.

Variation 1

F1, F2, 1, 2 & 3 Work as for *Basic Peyote Stitch Tubular Flower*, but starting with 8 beads in the Foundation circle.

4 The petals are *Variation 7* of the *Square Stitch Cupped Flowers*.

Variation 2

F1, F2, 1, 2 & 3 Work as for *Basic Peyote Stitch Tubular Flower*, but starting with 12 beads in the Foundation circle.

4 The petals are *Variation 3* of the *Brick Stitch Blossom Flowers*.

Flower first, then tube

There are occasions when it is useful to add a tubular section to the back of a flower you have already made. For example, it might simply not have occurred to you when planning the flower, to make it a tubular one. Or, for some of the flowers where there is a lot going on at the centre, it might be too fiddly to get the petals started from a tubular base. This is also a great way to give your flower a calyx or stem as we have done with several in the *Flower Collection*.

Adding a Herringbone Tube

To make a tubular section of *Herringbone* at the back of a flower, weave back to the circle of beads at its centre and bring the needle through any one of them. Then work around the circle as follows:

1 (Pick up 2, miss 1, go through 1) as many times as you need to work right round the circle, eg 4 times if there are 8 beads in the circle. Step up at the end of the round by going through the 1st bead picked up.

2 Now work in *Tubular Herringbone*: * pick up 2 and pass down into the bead below and up the adjacent bead. Continue around, repeating from *. Step up at the end of the row.

Repeat Row 2 until the tube is the length you require.

3 To draw the tube in at the end to finish, place 1 bead on the top of each rib. Work around again, placing 1 bead between each of the beads just added. Go through the new beads once more and pull them together neatly and firmly.

Adding a Peyote Stitch Tube

To make a tubular section of *Peyote Stitch* at the back of a flower, weave back to the circle of beads at its centre and bring the needle through any one of them. Then work around the circle as follows:

1 (Pick up 1, miss 1, go through 1) as many times as you need to work right round the circle, eg 4 times if there are 8 beads in the circle. Step up at the end of the round by going through the 1st bead picked up.

2 Now work in *Tubular Peyote Stitch*: * pick up 1, go through the next bead added in the previous round. Repeat from * around the circle and step up at the end of the round.

Repeat Row 2 until the tube is the length you require.

Variation 5 of the Peyote Stitch Filigree Flowers with a Herringbone Tube worked on to it.

Example 1 :
Basic Peyote Stitch Circular Flower and Variations with a Peyote Tube added to each.

Example 2 :
The petals are Variation 6 of the Peyote Filigree Flower. They were worked in size 15 seed beads from a Foundation circle of size 11 seed beads. The larger beads were then also used for the tube.

PART 2

THE FLOWER COLLECTION

On the following pages are a selection of popular flowers made using the stitches from the

Stitch Primer. Although some stitches lend themselves to certain shapes and directions, they are

not mutually exclusive, and in a couple of instances you will find the same flower made twice,

with different stitches. We hope this will encourage you to experiment for yourselves, either by

using your favourite stitches as a starting point, or by letting nature be your inspiration.

But remember, you don't have to be too literal, too botanically correct – you are creating your

interpretation and it must please you – fancy a purple rose or a fantasy flower?

Tulip SQUARE STITCH

Both the flower and its name originate in the Middle East but when tulips were brought to Europe in the late 16th Century, enthusiasm for the flowers amongst the Dutch upper classes triggered a speculative frenzy now known as Tulip Mania, with tulip bulbs considered a form of currency and exchanged for land, valuable livestock, and houses.

FIDDLY FACTOR

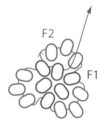

cylinder

SHOPPING LIST

seed beads in either size 11 or 15,
or cylinders, in green (G)
and petal colour (P)

Foundation

F1 Pick up 6 green beads, run through all the beads again and the next two or three beads once more, taking care not to split the thread. Do not knot.

F2 (Pick up 3P, miss 1, go through 1) 3 times. Go through the next green bead on the inner circle.

F3 (Pick up 2P, miss 1 green bead on the inner circle, go through the next green bead) 3 times. Go through the first 2P beads added in the round

The groups of 3 beads will form the base of the outer petals of the flower and the pairs of beads will form the base of the inner petals. Start by working on the inner petals.

Inner petals

1 Increase by 1 on each edge (4 beads).

2 Increase by 1 bead in the centre of the row (5 beads).

3 Decrease by 1 bead in the centre of the row (4 beads)

4 Work straight.

5 & 6 Decrease by 1 bead in the centre of each row (3 & 2 beads).

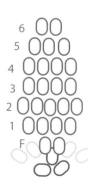

Weave down as described in Step 7 of the *Basic Square Stitch Flower*.

Make two more inner petals.

Go through the next green bead of the inner circle and the first group of 3 P beads of the Foundation.

Outer petals

1 Stitch 2 beads on to each bead (6 beads)

2 Increase by 1 bead in the centre of the row (7 beads).

3 - 6 Work as Rows 3 – 6 of the inner petals (6, 6, 5, & 4 beads)

7 Work straight.

8 Decrease by 1 in the centre of the row (3 beads).

Weave down as described in step 7 of the *Basic Square Stitch Flower*.

Make two more outer petals.

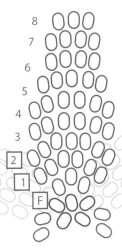

Stem (*Optional*)

1 Use green beads the same size as you have used for the petals. Stitch 2 beads between each alternate bead of the inner circle (6 beads). Work in *Tubular Herringbone* as described on *page 50* for 2 rows.

2 Change to a smaller bead and continue in *Tubular Herringbone* until the stem is the length you require.

Stamens

We have used black beads for the stamens in the centre of the

We found that *Square Stitch* was perfect to achieve the shaping we wanted for the petals. If you would prefer a more gentle curve, work one straight row in between Rows 2 and 3.

Size 11

Fuchsia HERRINGBONE & BRICK STITCHES

This extremely decorative pendulous flower is named after the 16th century botanist Fuchs. It is known as 'Our Lady's Eardrops' because the flowers resemble pendant earrings. There are many different varieties with varying lengths of sepals and petals. Once you have tried our version have a go at making the sepals and stamens longer, or the petals fuller.

FIDDLY FACTOR

SHOPPING LIST

seed beads in either size 11 or 15, or cylinders, in two colours green seed beads of a similar size and small drops for the stamens with one or two larger seed beads to fill the tube

Foundation and tubular section

F & 1 The Foundation and 1st Row of the tubular section at the top of the flower are worked the same as F & 1 of the *Basic Herringbone Daisy Flower* on *page 12*, but starting with only 8 beads.

2 To start working in tubular herringbone, * pick up 2 and pass down into the bead below and up the adjacent bead. Continue around, repeating from *. Step up at the end of the row.

3, 4, 5, 6, 7 & 8 Work as Row 2.

(For more guidance on working *Tubular Herringbone, see page 50*)

The sepals

Now change to *Brick Stitch* and work one sepal at a time.

9 Pick up 2 beads and pass the needle under the thread joining the top of the beads in the previous row and back up through the 2nd bead. Pull gently so that the two beads sit correctly. Pick up 1 bead and pass the needle under the same thread as before and back up through the bead just added. Jiggle the three beads so that they sit correctly. (You should have 3 beads on this row.) Turn.

10 Pick up 2 beads onto the 1st loop, and 2 beads onto the 2nd loop – worked individually (total 4 beads). Turn.

11 Pick up 2 beads on to the 1st loop, 1 on to the 2nd loop, and 2 on to the 3rd loop (total 5 beads). Turn.

12 Increase by 1 bead at the end of the row (6 beads).

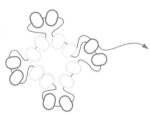
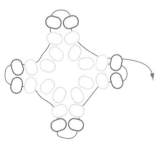

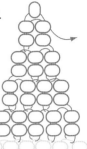

13, 14, 15 & 16 Work in *2-drop Brick Stitch* for the rest of the petal, adding 2 beads per stitch. Decrease by 1 stack of 2 beads at the beginning of each row, finishing with 1 bead on the top to make a picot point.

Needle down one side of the diamond (pulling gently to encourage a slight curve inwards) and weave through to the next pair of beads ready to start the next sepal.

Continue around to make 4 sepals in all.

If you wish to add more shaping to the finished flower then needle all the way around the outside edge of each sepal, pulling very gently. Work back to the tail thread and knot, then weave in and bury the ends.

2-drop Brick Stitch

Brick Stitch can be speeded up and elongated by using a number of beads as though they were a single bead. Using 2 beads per stitch is called *2-drop Brick Stitch*.

With ordinary *Brick Stitch*, each row starts with 2 beads to hide the thread. So, in *2-drop*, you need to pick up pick up 4 beads at the beginning of the row and go back up through the 3rd and 4th beads. Continue along the row picking up 2 beads each stitch.

Remember, when decreasing at the beginning of a row, to work the reinforcement described in the *Basic Brick Stitch Flower* on *page 20 (General notes)*. When doing this in *2-drop Brick Stitch*, you add 4 beads on the first loop first in *Square Stitch* and then work the 3rd and 4th beads again in *Brick Stitch*. This is not shown in the diagram illustrating Rows 13 – 16.

Inner petals

Make the inner frilly petals of the fuchsia entirely separately. Choose a contrasting colour and pick up 8 beads and turn into a circle. Knot. Pass through the 1st bead and add 7. Pass through the next 2 beads on the circle. Continue around in the same manner. Then add 9 beads on to the same original circle of beads, and continue around. Finally add 11 beads on to the same circle and continue around.

Work back to the tail thread and knot again, then sew into place inside the fuchsia sepals with one or two stitches.

Then add the stamens: * pick up 7 beads then a drop bead. Turn and pass back up through the 7 beads, hook around the circle of beads on the frilly petal, and repeat from * another two times, varying the length of the stamen slightly. Weave in and bury the ends.

When you are ready to assemble the fuchsia pick up 5 beads for the stalk, then a larger bead (making sure that it is large enough to cover the tube), the flower, enough beads to fill the tube and give it substance, 5 beads, then a drop bead. Turn and pass all the way back up through the beads and flower and beads of the stalk.

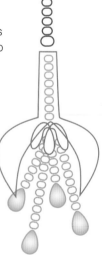

Daffodil SQUARE OR HERRINGBONE STITCH

Greek legend tells of a boy, Narcissus, who fell in love with his own reflection and wasted away. In his place grew a flower with white petals and a yellow centre. But to us, a daffodil is cheerful and optimistic, the harbinger of spring. There are many varieties of single and double flowers with all manner of petal and trumpet combinations. The Square Stitch Version is on a larger scale than the Herringbone.

FIDDLY FACTOR

Square Stitch Version

SHOPPING LIST

seed beads in either size 11 or 15, or cylinders, in green (G) and two other colours for the petals (P) and trumpet (T)

Foundation

Work as for *Tulip*.

Inner petals

1 Make as for *Square Stitch Flowers, Variation 2*. Make 2 more inner petals. Go through the next bead of the inner circle and the first group of 3 beads of the Foundation.

Outer petals

1 Increase by 1 in the centre of the row (4 beads).

2 - 9 As Steps 2 – 9 of *Square Stitch Flowers, Variation 2*. Make two more outer petals.

At the end of the third outer petal, weave down to Row 1. With the thread coming out at the edge of the petal and with the back of the flower facing you, * go through the 2 beads in the centre of Row 1 of the nearest inner petal. Now go through Row 1 of the next outer petal. Repeat from * twice so that you have connected all the inner and outer petals. Pull the thread up tight to cup the flower slightly and secure the thread so the flower will hold its shape.

Weave down to the inner circle and go through the 2 beads at the base of the nearest inner petal.

The trumpet

1 Stitch 1T to each of the beads at the base of the three inner petals (6 beads). Go through all of them once more to pull them into a circle.

2 Stitch 2T on to each bead (12 beads). Go through the first bead added in this round.

3 Work straight. Go through the first bead added in this round.

4 (Pick up 1T, go through 2) 6 times.

Stamens

Attach stamens by stitching into the beads at the centre of the trumpet or the beads of the Foundation.

Herringbone Stitch Version

Our *Herringbone Stitch Daffodil* combines the *Circular* form of the stitch for the petals with *Tubular Herringbone* for the trumpet.

SHOPPING LIST

seed beads in either size 11 or 15, or cylinders

FIDDLY FACTOR

We have given three different styles for the trumpets and used *Herringbone Stitch Daisy Flowers* for the petals – you might care to choose different variations. They can all be 'mix and matched'. The centre trumpets are left hollow to be filled in with stamens when you are ready to fix them onto your chosen backing.

The petals

1 Follow the instructions for your chosen *Herringbone Stitch Daisy Flower* – but knot at the beginning on the Foundation Row (to keep the base firm for working the trumpet later). We have used *Variations 1, 3 & 5* in making our daffodils.

2 Weave back to the Foundation Row, and start all over again to make the trumpet.

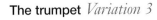

The trumpet *Variation 1*

1 * pick up 2 and pass through the next two beads. Continue around, repeating from *. Step up at the end of the row. Be very careful to ensure that all these beads are sitting correctly, and that the thread has not become caught up or twisted.

2 * pick up 2 and pass down into the bead below and up the adjacent bead. Continue around, repeating from *. Step up at the end of the row.

3, 4 & 5 Work as Row 2.

6 Work as Row 2 but add 1 extra bead on to each rib and 1 extra bead between each rib.

With Variation 3 of the Herringbone Stitch Daisy Flowers

With Variation 4 of the Herringbone Stitch Daisy Flowers

The trumpet *Variation 2*

1 & 2 Work as Rows 1 & 2 of *Variation 1* above.

3 Work as Row 2 but add 1 extra bead on to each rib and 1 extra bead between each rib.

With Variation 1 of the Herringbone Stitch Daisy Flowers

The trumpet *Variation 3*

1 & 2 Work as Rows 1 & 2 of *Variation 1* above.

3, 4, 5, 6 & 7 Work as Row 2.

8 Work as Row 2 but add 1 extra bead on to each rib and 1 extra bead between each rib.

Combinations of petals and trumpets using different colour schemes

Cornflower SQUARE STITCH

The annual blue cornflower is a slender plant of great charm and was a central symbol of romanticism, standing for desire and love.

The petals are worked in Square Stitch sitting atop a neat little 'covered bead' calyx. Bugle beads seemed to suit the stamens for this flower but you can of course do any of the stamen variations you fancy.

FIDDLY FACTOR

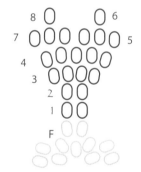

Size 11

Size 15

SHOPPING LIST

seed beads in either size 11 or 15, or cylinders, in blue for the petals and brown for the calyx a few 6 mm bugles (or longer) for the stamens 1 x size 6 seed bead, brown

Foundation

Work as for *Basic Square Stitch Flower* but start with 12 beads.

Outer petals

1 & 2 Work straight (2 beads).

3 - 8 Work as Rows 1 - 6 of *Square Stitch Flowers, Variation 5*.

9 Weave down as Step 7 of the *Basic Square Stitch Flower*.

Make 5 more outer petals. Finish by bringing the thread through one of the beads of the inner circle.

Inner petals

1 Stitch 2 beads on to the single bead of the inner circle.

2 - 7 As Rows 1 - 6 of *Square Stitch Flowers, Variation 5*.

8 Weave down as before, bringing the thread out through the next bead of the inner circle.

Make 11 more inner petals. You will find that six of the inner petals will sit immediately in front of the outer petals; the other six will sit in between these two sets of petals, forming a middle layer.

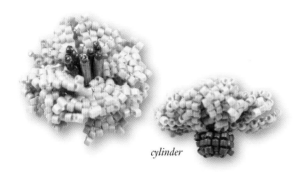

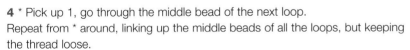

cylinder

In folklore, cornflowers were worn by young men in love. If the flower faded too quickly, it was taken as a sign that the man's love was unrequited – if only they had had a beaded flower!

Calyx

Hold the flower upside down so that you are looking down on the inner circle of beads.

1 Stitch 1 brown bead on to every alternate bead of the circle (6 beads), ending with the thread coming out of any of the new beads.

2 Pick up 7 brown beads and go through the bead the thread is coming from and on through the next brown bead added in Step 1.

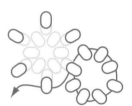

3 Repeat Step 2 until there are six loops of brown beads. Go through 4 beads of the first loop again so that the thread is coming out of the middle bead.

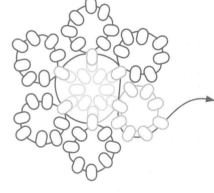

4 * Pick up 1, go through the middle bead of the next loop.
Repeat from * around, linking up the middle beads of all the loops, but keeping the thread loose.

5 Place a size 6 seed bead (or similar) over the space at the centre of the flower and then pull the thread tight so that the brown beads gather around the large bead. Jiggle the bead to make sure that its hole lines up with the space in the centre of the inner circle. Secure the thread while everything is pulled up tight.

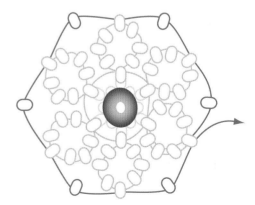

Stamens

Stitch bugle bead stamens in the centre of the flower, each time going down through the large bead and anchoring the thread through one of the brown beads of the calyx.

Iris HERRINGBONE & SQUARE STITCHES

In Greek legend Iris was the messenger of the gods and her path through the heavens was visible by the rainbow she left in her wake – the iris is associated with a myriad of colours – hence the word iridescent. These lovely iris, reminiscent of Japanese Water Iris, are made in Herringbone and Square Stitch, and offer great scope for colour shading of beads.

FIDDLY FACTOR

cylinder

Size 11

SHOPPING LIST

seed beads in either size 11 or cylinders

seed beads in size 15 in a contrast
colour for the beard

green 3mm bugles or similar for the style

F (Foundation Row): Pick up 6 beads and turn into a circle *(see the notes in Tips & Techniques Section on pages 8 & 9)*. Knot.

1 & 2 Repeat Rows 1 and 2 from the *Basic Herringbone Stitch Daisy Flower*.

3 Place 2 beads on to the rib and 2 beads between each rib.

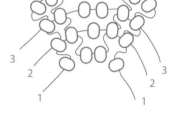

4 *Place 2 beads on to the rib. Pass through the bead below and then the 1st of the 2 new beads added to make the new rib and pick up 4. Pass down into the next new bead and follow the thread path up and pass up into the next rib. Continue around from *. (i.e. 2 onto an old rib and 4 onto a new rib.)

5 Place 4 beads onto each rib, passing the thread all the way down the rib each time and then up again, so that each rib is totally separate.

The petals should, with a little encouragement, fall into the shape required, but if they need extra tweaking, then run a thread around the outside of the petals and pull gently.

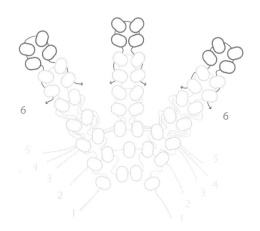

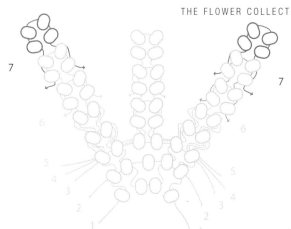

6 Repeat the previous row.

7 Repeat the previous row for 3 alternate petals. For the other 3 petals pass through the ribs without adding any extra beads.

(In the diagrams above, the thread path for Rows 6 and 7 is only shown at the top of the ribs, not along the sides.)

Now change to *Square Stitch*.

Work the petals one at a time, firstly the 3 longer ribs which will be the 'falls' and then the shorter ribs – the 'standards':

> *Key to the diagrams:* square stitch beads ◯
> embellishing beads ◯ ◯

Falls

Place 5 beads on each side of the rib, *(see the Square Stitch instructions on page 28)* and then 3 beads. *Slip Stitch* an additional 2 beads on each side of the petal as in the diagram. Change to a tiny bead (size 15) to work the 'beard'. *Slip Stitch* a tiny bead in the centre of the rib between each row of beads for 6 rows, pull gently to encourage the petal to arch slightly. Pass the thread around the outside of the petal and across the base beads of the shorter rib (pulling gently to encourage the correct shape) to start the next 'fall'. Repeat twice.

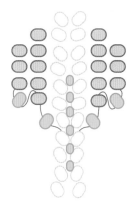

Standards

Place 3 beads on each side of the rib *(see the Square Stitch instructions on page 28)*. *Slip Stitch* an additional 1 bead on the end as in the diagram. Pass the thread around the outside of the petal and across the base beads of the 'fall' (pulling gently to encourage the correct shape) to start the next 'standard'. Repeat twice.

When you are ready to attach the flower to your work, add the 'style' in the centre of the petals:

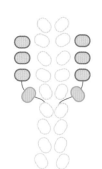

Style

Pick up 2 small bugles (3mm) and 1 tiny bead. *Pass back down the 2 bugles to the central ring of beads and hook the thread around it. Pass back up the 1st bugle, pick up 1 bugle and 1 tiny bead and repeat from * until there is a branch of 3 bugles. Work back to the tail thread, and knot again and weave in and bury ends.

Snowdrop HERRINGBONE OR SQUARE STITCH

Legend has it that, after the expulsion of Eve from the Garden of Eden, no flowers bloomed and snow fell ceaselessly. An Angel, comforting Eve, caught a snowflake in his hand, breathed on it and it fell to earth as the first snowdrop. Do we all go searching for that first sight of the milky white snowdrop peeping through the snow or the undergrowth – to take heart that winter is coming to an end?

FIDDLY FACTOR

Size 11

Size 15

SHOPPING LIST

seed beads in either size 11 or 15,
or cylinders, in green and white

Herringbone Stitch Version

Foundation and Rows 1 - 4

Use green beads. Starting with 6 beads, make a *Herringbone* tube as described in the *Tubular Flowers* section on *page 50.*

5 Change to white beads and work 1 row.

6 Pick up 4 beads instead of 2 on to each rib (this is *2-drop Herringbone Stitch*) and place 1 bead between the ribs. Repeat around.

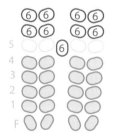

This beautifully delicate snowdrop has petals that you can manipulate to turn either up or down – you could also vary the length of the petals and the inner frill.

7 Pick up 4 beads instead of 2, pass through the beads immediately below, and through the new centre bead and into the next rib (i.e. following the previous thread path), and continue around in the same manner.

8 Pick up 5 beads onto the rib, and follow the previous thread path.

Needle up through Row 5 and the top layer of Row 6, and with the needle exiting from the top of the 3rd white bead on the rib, *Square Stitch* along the side of the rib for 5: pick up 1 and pass back up through the bead on the rib in a circular motion and up the next. * Pick up 1 and pass down the last new bead and up the adjacent bead on the rib and the next two above. Repeat from * until there are 5 new beads on the side of the rib.

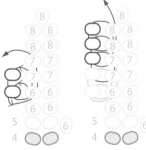

Needle around so that the needle is exiting from the top-side new bead.
Pick up 1 and pass into the centre-top.
Pick up 3 and pass again in a circular motion through centre-top (creating a picot), and continue along through the top bead on the opposite side.

Pick up 1 and pass through the same bead again in a circular motion and the one below.

Pick up 1 and pass up the new bead just added previously and down what was the top-side bead of the rib and across the rib and up the original other top-side bead of the rib (where there was not previously a joining thread). Pass through what was the centre-top bead, pick up 1 and pass down the 2 new side beads.

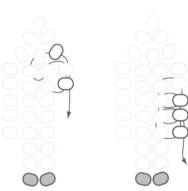

Continue to *Square Stitch* down the side of the rib to make a total of 5 beads.

Pass into the centre bead added between the ribs in Row 6. Pick up 2 beads and pass back through the centre bead in a circular motion (these beads will form the bottom of the inner frill of smaller petals). Pass into the next rib and continue around in the same manner, making two more petals by adding the extra beads to the centre beads between the ribs.

Needle through to exit out of the 1st bead of a newly formed rib.

7A Pick up 2 beads and add onto the rib and pass into the next new rib.
Repeat around, pulling the thread to make these petals form inside the longer petals.

8A Pick up 2 beads and add onto the rib and repeat around, following the previous thread path to separate the petals.

9A Change to green beads and repeat Row 8A.

Change to white beads and with the needle exiting between the white and green beads, *Square Stitch* 2 beads onto the side, and then place 2 beads on the top, and finally *Square Stitch* 2 beads down the other side.

Repeat around for the other two inner petals.

Needle through to the beginning thread. Pull the beginning tail tight and knot the two threads together and bury the ends.

Square Stitch Version

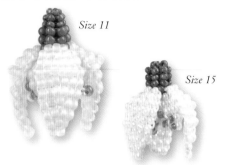

Size 11

Size 15

SHOPPING LIST

seed beads in either size 11 or 15,

or cylinders, in green and white

Foundation

Work as *Tulip*, using white beads as the P beads.

Inner petals

1 Using white beads and working in *Square Stitch* increase by 1 on each edge (4 beads).

2 Increase by 1 bead at each edge and in the centre of the row, placing a green bead in the middle of the row (7 beads).

3 Stitch 1 bead on to each of the first 2 beads and 1 green bead on to the 3rd bead. Turn.

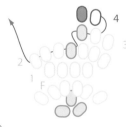

4 Stitch 1 green bead on to the green bead added in the previous row and 1 bead on to the next bead. Go through the 2 beads immediately below the beads just added. Continuing in the same direction, go through the green bead of the row below (2nd Row) and the 3 white beads to exit the edge of the petal.

5 & 6 Work as Rows 3 & 4 on the left hand side of the petal.

7 Stitch through the 1st Row and the 2 Foundation beads once more. Go through the next bead on the inner circle of beads and the next set of 2 white beads added in the Foundation.

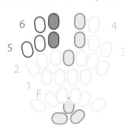

Make two more inner petals.

Go through the next green bead of the inner circle and the first group of 3 white beads of the Foundation.

Outer petals

1 - 3 Work as Rows 1 – 3 of *Square Stitch Flower, Variation 4* (5, 6 & 7 beads).

4 Decrease by 1 bead in the centre of the row (6)

5 Work straight.

6 - 9 Decrease by 1 bead in the centre of each row, concluding with 2 beads at the tip of the petal.

10 Work as Step 10 of *Square Stitch Flower, Variation 3*.

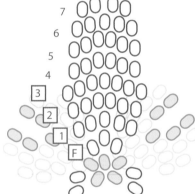

Make two more outer petals.

Calyx

1 Use green beads the same size as you have used for the petals. Stitch 2 beads between each alternate bead of the inner circle (6 beads). Work in *Tubular Herringbone* as described on *page 50* for 1 row.

2 Change to a smaller bead (unless you are already working in the smallest you have). Continue in *Tubular Herringbone* for 2 rows.

3 Pick up 1 bead on each rib and go through them to pull them into a tight circle.

Pink HERRINGBONE & SQUARE STITCHES

The group of flowers known as dianthus (from the Greek dios – divine/god, and anthos – flower) includes all the pinks and carnations. The pink is the quintessential cottage garden flower, fragrant and ornamental, and the colour pink is named after it. Our pinks are made using a combination of Herringbone and Square Stitch, and there are two different flowers to try – start with the single before progressing to the more fiddly double.

FIDDLY FACTOR

SHOPPING LIST

seed beads size 11 or cylinders in pink and green
seed beads size 15 in a contrasting or toning pink

Single Pink

F & 1 Using green beads, work as Rows F and 1 from the *Basic Circular Herringbone Stitch Flower*.

2 * Pick up 2 and pass down into the bead below and up the adjacent bead. Continue around, repeating from *. Step up at the end of the row.

3 - 5 Place the work onto a cocktail stick or cotton wool bud (or any suitable form of the correct size) and pull the thread gently whilst pressing the beads into a tubular shape. Continue straight, repeating Row 2.

Change to pink beads:
6 Repeat Row 2.

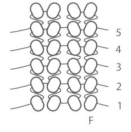

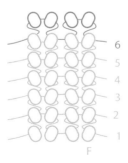

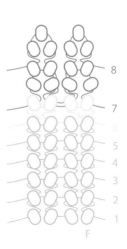

7 Pick up 4 beads instead of 2.

8 Pick up 3 beads instead of 2 or 4, and needle down to Row 7 and up again into the next rib (to form the petals).

Rows 7A, 7B & 8A

a With the needle exiting from the top of the 1st bead of Row 7, pick up 1 and pass back up the same bead and up into the next bead.

b Pick up 1 and pass down the new bead just added, and then up the two rib beads and up the next rib bead.

c Add a further bead and pass down the bead immediately below and then up two beads of the rib, and through the picot bead on the top.

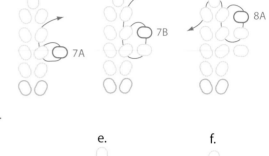

d, e, f Work down the other side of the petal in the same manner so that there are 3 new beads added on to the side of the rib. Pass to the next petal and continue around in the same manner.

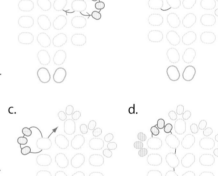

Change to size 15 seed beads and again finish one petal before moving onto the next:

a With the needle exiting the top of the rib (Row 8), pick up 3 beads and pass down the side bead. Pick up 3 beads and go through the side bead again in a circular motion. Pass back up through the top rib bead and through the top picot bead.

b Add 3 beads and go through the picot bead again in a circular motion, and then down into the top of the rib on the other side and up the end side bead.

c Pick up 3 beads and pass back up the end bead in a circular motion.

d Pick up 3 beads and pass down the adjacent rib-bead and all the way down the rib and up into the next rib to continue around in the same manner.

When all the petals are finished, needle down to the beginning thread. Pull gently but firmly on the beginning tail end to tighten the row and pull the shape in and then knot.

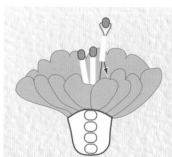

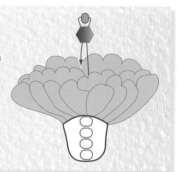

Tip

The tubular base of the flower is quite wide. So, when you are ready to attach the flower (either a *single* or *double* Pink) to your project by adding the stamens of your choice, you first need to add large enough beads inside the tube to block the opening.

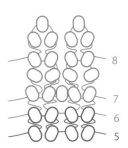

Double Pink

First layer

Work as the *Single Pink* but on Row 7 add 1 bead between each rib (then continue as before, ignoring the new bead).

Second layer (outside)

When the first layer of petals are completed, return to Row 5 (green) on the outside of the petals, and pass through the 1st bead (so that the new petals will be staggered from the first layer). Repeat the entire sequence of petals again (without adding the single extra beads).

Third layer (inside)

Needle through to an extra bead added on Row 7 of the first layer (which will be the base for another set of petals).
Working on the inside of the petals, pick up 2 beads and pass through the extra bead again in a circular motion.
Needle through the 2 adjacent rib beads of Row 7 to the next extra bead and continue around in the same manner.

When the row is completed pass into the 1st of the 2 new beads added (this is a new rib).

Now finish one petal at a time before moving on to the next:

a Pick up 3 beads and pass down into the 2nd of the new beads added.

b Pass back up the 1st bead in a circular motion and pick up 1 bead. Pass back up the same bead in a circular motion and up to the top of the rib.

c Pick up 1 bead and pass down the newest bead added and back up the two beads of the rib. Pass through the top picot bead and down the 1st top bead of the rib.

d Pick up 1 bead and pass around in a circular motion, and on down through the bottom bead of the rib.

e Pick up 1 bead and pass up through the new bead just added, down the top bead of the rib and back up the top end bead.

a.   b.   c.   d.   e.

Change to size 15 seed beads and add the frilly edging to the petals in the same way as before.

When all the petals are finished, needle down to the beginning thread. Pull gently but firmly on the beginning tail end to tighten the row and pull the shape in and then knot.

71

Peony HERRINGBONE STITCH & RIGHT ANGLE WEAVE

The traditional floral symbol of China, the peony has been cultivated for over 2000 years and the flower denotes luxury and indulgence. These luscious flowers are made in Herringbone Stitch with additions in a variation of Right Angle Weave. The flowers are shaded in three colours to give extra interest (and also to make them easier to work!)

FIDDLY FACTOR
🌼🌼 🌼🌼 🌼🌼 🌼

SHOPPING LIST

3 shades (light, medium, dark) of seed beads
in either size 11 or 15, or cylinders

Key to the diagrams: dark coloured beads ⭘
medium coloured beads ◍
light coloured beads ⭘

Inner layer

F & 1 The Foundation and 1st Row are worked the same as F & 1 of the *Basic Herringbone Stitch Daisy Flower* on *page 12*.

2 * pick up 2 and pass down into the bead below and up the adjacent bead. Continue around, repeating from * and keeping the tension tight so that the ribs begin to form a tube. Step up at the end of the row.

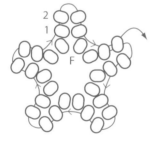

3 Work as Row 2, but placing 3 beads onto the rib instead of 2, pulling the ribs firmly together into a cup shape. Do not step up at the end of this row.

Change to medium coloured beads to work a frilly edge around each petal.

4 With the needle exiting from the top of a Row 2 bead, pick up 3 and pass back through the Row 2 bead in a circular motion, and up through the Row 3 bead.

5 Pick up 2 beads and pass through the 1st of the new beads just put on and back up through the Row 3 bead and the next bead.

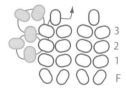

6 Repeat Step 5 three more times so that 5 beads are edged, and step across and up into the Row 1 bead of the next rib. Repeat this process on

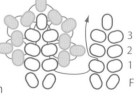

all five petals. You will find that the edging beads will curve backwards, sitting around the outside of the 'cup' shape.

After the final addition of edging beads, step into the next rib by going down through the nearest Row 1 bead and continue through the F bead and then up through the next F and Row 1 bead, on the OUTSIDE of the work.

Middle layer

2A Work in dark beads. Pick up 2 beads and pass the needle down into the next bead in the adjacent rib to form the base of the 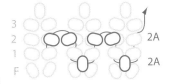 first petal of the middle layer. Pick up 1 bead and pass up into the next available bead of Row 1. Continue around the petals in the same manner, taking care to keep all the petals of the inner layer gathered closely together in the centre of the work as you go around the outside. Step up at the end of the round by going through the 1st bead added. Note – the edging beads of the inner layer are not shown in the diagrams for the middle layer.

Change to medium coloured beads.

3A Add 4 beads onto each rib and, following the thread path, pass the needle through the new single bead added in the previous row.
Repeat around and step up at the end of the round by going through the first 2 beads added.

Change to light coloured beads.

4A Add 3 beads onto each rib and, following the thread path, pass the needle down through all the beads of the rib and go through the same single bead between each one.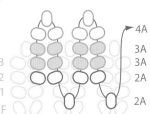

Work a frilly edge around each petal:

5A Start with the needle exiting from the top of a LOWER Row 3A bead, pick up 3 and pass back through the same bead in a circular motion, and up through the UPPER Row 3A bead.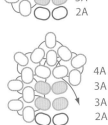

6A Continue as for the inner layer until you have added edging to 5 beads of the petal, ending with your thread exiting the 3rd bead added in Row 4A.

7A Pass again through the two new beads added and pick up 1 bead (of either light or medium colour); pass through the adjacent top bead, pick up 1 bead and pass through the next two outside beads and then reverse and pass up around the original 3 top beads added in Row 4A.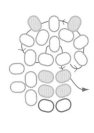

8A Continue down the petal, adding edging beads to the next two beads so that 7 beads in all are edged. Have the frill curving upwards and inwards towards the centre of the flower.

Outer layer

The outer layer of petals is worked identically to the middle layer.

To set the base of the petals, bring the needle up through an F bead sitting underneath and to the left of one of the single beads added in Row 2A. * Pick up 2, go down through the next F bead. Pick up 1, go up through the next F bead. Repeat from * 4 times.

Work a petal on to each of the five pairs of beads, passing through the single bead to go from one petal to the next.

This design could also be used as a rose, or as the starting point for many other double flowers, such as camellias and dahlias, depending on the colours and the central stamens, and the tips of the petals.

Orchid PEYOTE STITCH

Flamboyant and exotic, these are the largest family of plants in the world. By reputation difficult to grow, yet they frequently appear in shops nowadays alongside more commonplace houseplants. Our orchids are worked in Peyote Stitch and there are two versions for you to choose from for the upper petals – gently rounded or flying out at odd angles. The lower petal is worked last and is the same for both versions.

FIDDLY FACTOR

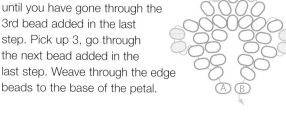

Version 1, size 11

Version 1, cylinder

Version 1, size 15

SHOPPING LIST

seed beads in either size 11 or 15, or cylinders:
one main colour for the upper petals plus a few in a lighter shade;
and a second main colour for the lower petal,
plus 5 contrasting beads.

Foundation

Use the colour of beads you will use for the upper petals.

F1 Pick up 8 beads, run through all the beads again and the next two or three beads once more, taking care not to split the thread. Do not knot.

F2 (Pick up 2, miss 1, go through 1) 3 times. Pass through the next three beads of the inner circle of beads.

F3 Counting only beads of the inner circle, (pick up 2, miss 1, go through 1) twice. Go up through the 6th bead added in step F2, pointing towards the 5th bead added. Treat these beads as Beads A and B of the first upper petal.

Upper petals, Version 1

1, 2 & 3 Work as Steps 1, 2 & 3 of *Basic Peyote Stitch Flower.*

Work Steps 4 & 5 in a lighter shade to highlight the edges of the petal.

4 Go up through Bead A, the next two beads and the 1st bead added in the last step. Pick up 2, go through 1. Go through the next two beads on the edge of the petal. (Pick up 1, go through 1) twice. Go through the next two beads. Pick up 2, go through 1, the next two beads and Bead B.

5 Go through Bead A and weave through the edge beads of the petal until you have gone through the 3rd bead added in the last step. Pick up 3, go through the next bead added in the last step. Weave through the edge beads to the base of the petal.

Upper petals, Version 2

Work as for *Variation 2* of *Peyote Stitch Flower.*

For both versions, work an upper petal on each of the four remaining pairs of beads of the Foundation.

Two of the upper petals will sit in front of the other three upper petals.

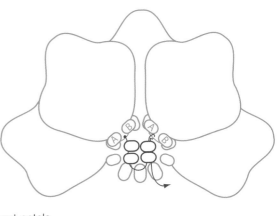

Lower petal

To make the base of the lower petal:

Weave through the inner circle of beads to the base of one of the
two upper petals which is sitting in front of the other three.
Knot the thread to the loops of thread between Beads A and
B of the petal.

Pick up 4 beads and pass the needle behind the loops of
thread between Beads A and B of the other petal at the front of
the flower. Go through the 4th and 3rd beads just picked up.
Pull up tightly so that the four new beads sit in between the two front petals
with the bead holes facing downwards. Stitch around all four new beads again
to reinforce them. They form the base of the lower petal. Treat the pair of beads
your thread is coming from as Bead A of the lower petal and the pair of beads
sitting next to it as bead B. (In subsequent working, stitch through each of
these pairs of beads as though they were one bead.)

To make the body of the Lower Petal:

1 Work as Step 1 of *Basic Peyote Stitch Flower*, picking up the 11 beads in
this colour sequence: 3 Main, 5 Contrast, 3 Main.

2 & 3 Work as Steps 2 & 3 of *Variation 1 Peyote Stitch Flower* (all main
colour beads).

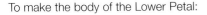

4 Go through Bead A and the next seven beads along the edge.
Pick up 1, go through 1. (Pick up 2, go through 1) twice. Pick up 1, go through 1.

5 Turn by hooking around the thread and go back through 2 beads.
(Pick up 1, go through 2) twice. Pick up 1, go through 1.

6 Turn and go back through 2. (Pick up 1, go through 1)
twice. Pull up gently to start to form the 'lip' of the petal.

7 Turn and go back through
two. Pick up 2, go through
1 to fill the centre of the
'lip'. Continue around all
the edge beads, pulling
them tight together.

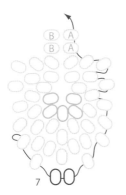

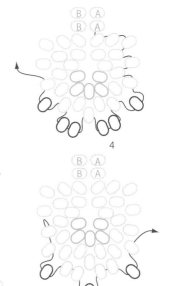

Version 2, size 15

Version 2, cylinder

Version 2, size 11

Columbine SQUARE & PEYOTE STITCHES

The columbine is a delightful and graceful cottage garden plant, holding its intricate flowers on fine stems above the foliage. Each flower has five spurs that contain nectar to attract pollinating birds and bees. Our columbine is worked in a combination of Square and Peyote Stitches. Take extra care with the Foundation for this flower as it is worked rather differently from the others – study the thread path in the diagrams in particular.

FIDDLY FACTOR

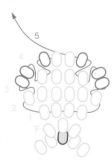

Size 15

SHOPPING LIST

seed beads in either size 11 or 15, or cylinders, in three colours:

Rear Petals (R) ◯   Front Petals (F) ◯   Calyx (C) ◯

Foundation

a Pick up 1R, 2F 5 times and tie in a circle. Go through the F next to the knot.

b Pick up 3F, turn and come back through the next F bead from the opposite side of it and the bead the thread is coming out of, missing out the R bead between them.

c * Go through the next 2F, missing the R bead between them. Pick up 3F and go through the 2F again.

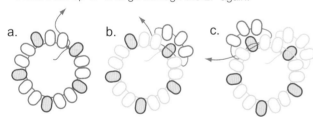

a.   b.   c.

Repeat from * 3 times. Go through the last 3F again.

cylinder

Inner petals

Work each inner petal separately in *Square Stitch* on to the groups of 3F beads. Do not worry if the Foundation beads swivel around as you make the inner petals – you can settle them all into the right place before starting on the Calyx.

1 Increase by 1 in the centre of the row. (4 beads)

2 Increase by 1 bead on each edge (6)

3 Decrease by 1 bead on each edge (4)

4 Decrease by 1 bead on each edge (2)

5 Work as Step 6 of *Square Stitch Flower Variation 1* (ignoring the row numbers given there).

6 Weave down through the edge beads and the lower rows to the base of the petal and go through the next 2F beads on the inner circle (missing out the R between them) and through the 3F of the Foundation.

Make four more inner petals.

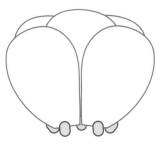

Calyx

Hold the inner petals together and make sure that the single R beads of the inner circle are all sitting around the outside of the base of the petals.

Now work in *Tubular Peyote Stitch*:

1 With the thread coming from a R bead, * pick up 2C and go through the next R. Repeat from * 4 times. Go through the 1st 2C picked up.

2 (Pick up 1C, go through 2C) 5 times. Go through the 1st C picked up.

3 (Pick up 1C, go through 1C) 5 times. Go through the 1st C picked up.

4 Pick up 1C, go through the next 2C) twice. Pick up 1C, go through 1C. Go through the 3C added in this round and pull them tightly together. Fasten off.

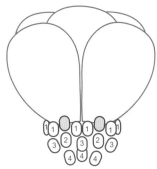

Outer petals

1 Foundation

Hold the flower with the inner petals uppermost and take the thread through one of the R beads of the inner circle, going from left to right. * Pick up 2R and go through the next R. Repeat from * 4 times. Go through the 1st R picked up. This is Bead A and the bead immediately to it's right is Bead B.

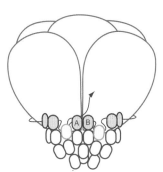

2 Petal – work five petals separately in *Peyote Stitch*:

Follow the instructions for the petal of *Peyote Stitch Flower Variation 5* (Steps 1 – 4). The diagram shows the first petal at the end of Step 4. Beads A and B will by now be sitting as shown and the thread will be exiting Bead B.

To make the spur of the petal:

a Pick up 4R and go up through Bead A. Turn and go back down through Bead B and the first 2 beads just added.

b Pick up 5R, miss the last bead picked up and go back through 4R, the 3rd and 4th beads added in the previous step and bead A. Turn and go down through Bead B once more.

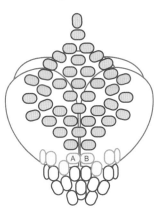

Go through the next R bead of the inner circle and the 1st bead of the next pair added in the Foundation.

Make four more outer petals.

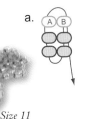

Size 11

a.

b.

PART 3

BUDS & GREENERY

Here are some gorgeous tiny flowers, flowerbuds and exquisite berries just perfect for adding into your projects; and green bits for leaves, tendrils and sepals (but of course they don't have to be green!). These little decorative motifs will set off the flowers to perfection, but don't be too dogmatic about using the correct colour – take a step back and use a colour that tones or complements the rest of your piece.

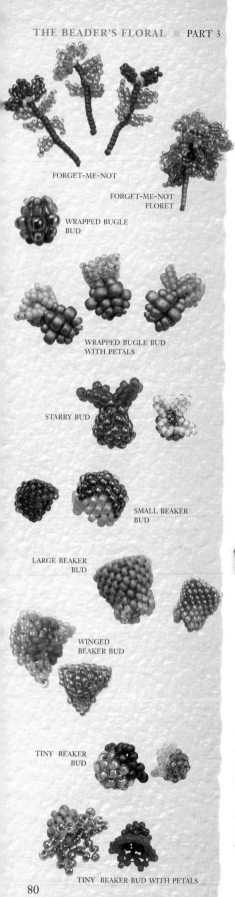

FORGET-ME-NOT

FORGET-ME-NOT
FLORET

WRAPPED BUGLE
BUD

WRAPPED BUGLE BUD
WITH PETALS

STARRY BUD

SMALL BEAKER
BUD

LARGE BEAKER
BUD

WINGED
BEAKER BUD

TINY BEAKER
BUD

TINY BEAKER BUD WITH PETALS

Buds & Tiny Flowers

Simple Four-Petalled Flower

FIDDLY FACTOR

SHOPPING LIST

beads in two sizes, medium (M) and small (S)

1 Pick up 4M, pass through them again and then knot into a circle. Pass through the first bead in the circle and * pick up 8S and pass back through the same M and then through the next M. Continue around from * until there are 4 petals.

2 ** Pass up the first S of the petal, pick up 2S and pass down the last S on that petal, through the M and the next M. Continue around repeating from ** until each of the 4 petals has been filled in. (You may need to press each petal between you finger and thumb to get the beads to lie in the correct place.)

3 Return to the beginning tail thread and knot the two ends together then weave and bury the threads.

Multi-Loop Flower

FIDDLY FACTOR

SHOPPING LIST

a few seed beads, all same size size,
or cylinders, in one colour for the centre (C)
and a second for the petals (P)

1 Pick up 3C and tie them into a circle. *Pick up 8 or 9P and pass directly into the next C. Pick up 8 or 9P and pass back through the same C again in a circular motion. Repeat from * twice to make 6 loops in all. The petals will not lie flat, but will twist and turn this way and that. (The diagram shows the two styles of loop in different shades, for clarity, but they are all worked in the same colour.)

2 Tie the two ends of thread together. Stitch one back into the flower and cut off. Use the other thread to make some stamens of your choice while attaching the flower to your project.

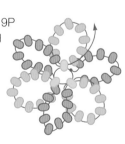

Tiny Ruffle Flower

FIDDLY FACTOR

SHOPPING LIST

a few seed beads (S)

Foundation

F Pick up 4S and go through all the beads again to turn them into a circle and knot.

1 Pass through the bead next to the knot then * pick up 3S and pass through the same bead of the Foundation in a circular motion. Pick up another 3S and go through the same bead again. Move to the next bead on the Foundation.

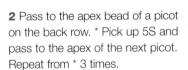

Repeat from * and continue around so that all of the 4 beads on the Foundation Row have two sets of 3 beads.

2 Pass to the apex bead of a picot on the back row. * Pick up 5S and pass to the apex of the next picot. Repeat from * 3 times.

3 Repeat Step 2, working either in front or behind that row so that all of the picots of Row 1 have a double ruffle on them.

Knot and weave in the ends.

Rose Ruffle Flower

FIDDLY FACTOR

SHOPPING LIST

a few seed beads (S)

This flower is based on the little Netted Ruffle used to create Double Flowers on page 49. Here it is used independently, instead of having a larger flower in the background.

Foundation

Pick up 10 beads and go through all the beads again to turn them into a circle, knot and pass through the bead next to the knot.

1 * Pick up 3 beads and pass through the next 2 beads in the Foundation circle. Repeat from * around the circle. Pass the needle up through the centre bead of the first group of 3 just added.

2, 3 & 4 Work as Steps 2, 3 & 4 of the *Netted Ruffle* on *page 49.*

You might like to stitch a 4 mm crystal across the centre of the flower.

Work back to the tail thread and knot again, then weave in and bury ends.

Variation

FIDDLY FACTOR

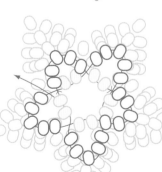

F, 1, 2, 3 & 4 Work as *Rose Ruffle Flower.*

Needle down to the Foundation circle to emerge from the edge of any pair of beads.

5 * Pick up 5 beads and pass through the next pair on the Foundation circle. Repeat from * 4 times. (There are five pairs on the circle, so that after the 1st two you will be looping around the earlier groups added – either in front or behind, it doesn't matter which.)

Forget-Me-Not

This little flower reminded us of the forget-me-not – diminutive on its own, but in a mass they can be a breathtaking sight in spring. Make several single-flowered stems or add lots of blooms to one stem as in Forget-Me-Not Floret.

SHOPPING LIST

seed beads size 15 for the stems (S), the leaves (L), the flower centres (FC) and petals (P)

FIDDLY FACTOR

1 Put on a stop bead and pick up 15 - 20 S.

2 Make a petal: pick up 1FC and 8 - 10 P and go back through the FC towards the stem. Go through 2S. Make a leaf by following the instructions for a sepal on *page 88*, picking up 5 or 6L.

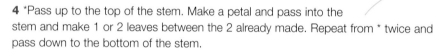

3 Go down through the all remaining S and remove the stop bead. Miss 1S and go up through the rest to about half way up the stem. Make another leaf.

4 *Pass up to the top of the stem. Make a petal and pass into the stem and make 1 or 2 leaves between the 2 already made. Repeat from * twice and pass down to the bottom of the stem.

5 Finish off both thread ends by passing through the S at the base of the stem and back up into the stem.

❖❖❖

Forget-Me-Not Floret

SHOPPING LIST

cylinders for the main stem (C)

seed beads size 15 for the side stems (S), the leaves (L), the flower centres (FC) and petals (P)

FIDDLY FACTOR

F1 Put on a stop bead and pick up 15 - 20 C for the main stem and 5S for a side stem.

2 Make a petal as for *Forget-Me-Not, above.*

3 Go through 2S. Make a leaf as for *Forget-Me-Not.* Go back up through the 2S to the top of the side stem. * Make a petal and go back down into the side stem a little lower than before. Make another leaf and go back to the top of the side stem. Repeat from * once more so there are three petals and three leaves.

4 Pass into the main stem and right down to the bottom of it. Remove the stop bead. Pick up 1S and go up through the C beads of the stem to about a third of the way up it. Make another leaf, a little larger this time (picking up 7 or 8L).

5 Pass up the main stem and emerge 1C lower than the previous side stem. Pick up 4 or 5 S for the next side stem and repeat Steps 2 & 3. Pass down into the main stem and make another leaf near the one added in Step 4.

6 Repeat Step 5 until you have made 5 or 6 sets of flowers. Add more leaves to the main stem if you wish and finish off both thread ends by passing through the S and back up into the main stem.

Wrapped Bugle Bud   FIDDLY FACTOR

SHOPPING LIST

1 x 6mm Bugle bead (B)

a few seed beads in size 8

(M for medium) in green and size 11

(S for small) and size 15 (T for tiny)

in green and a petal colour

1 Pick up 1B, * 1T, 1S, 1 M, 1S, 1T and pass back down through the B in a circular motion. Repeat from * four times so that there are 5 stacks of beads just covering the bugle. The first 3 beads picked up each time should be green.

2 Pass the needle up one of the stacks and knot the two ends together and bury the ends of thread.

Wrapped Bugle Bud with Petals   FIDDLY FACTOR

SHOPPING LIST

as above, all of the same colour, and a few seed beads

size 15 in a flower colour (F)

1 Work as Step 1 of *Wrapped Bugle Bud*.
Pass the needle up one of the stacks and knot the two ends together.

2 * Pick up 10 F and pass down the next-but-one stack of beads and then up the stack immediately behind. Continue around from * for a further 4 times so that there are a total of 5 petals. Knot the two ends together and bury the threads.

Starry Bud   FIDDLY FACTOR

SHOPPING LIST

seed beads size 11 or size 15 or cylinders in green (G)

and a petal colour (P)

1 Pick up 4 G, run through all the beads again and the next one or two beads once more, taking care not to split the thread. Do not knot.

Now work in *Peyote Stitch* as follows, 'stepping up' at the end of each row:

2 (Pick up 1G, go through the next bead) 4 times.

3 (Pick up 2G, go through 1) 4 times (8 beads added in all). At the end of the round, step up by going through the pair of beads added at the beginning.

4 (Pick up 1G, go through 2) 4 times.

5 & 6 Work as Steps 3 & 4.

7 & 8 (Pick up 1G, go through 1) 4 times. Don't pull these rows up too tightly for the moment.

9 (Pick up 2P, go through 1) 4 times.

10 * pick up 2P and pass down into the next bead and up the adjacent bead. Continue around, repeating from *. (This is *Tubular Herringbone Stitch*.)

11 * pick up 3P and pass down through the next bead and that below it and up the adjacent 2 beads. Continue around, repeating from *.

Needle back down to Rows 7 & 8 and pass through them again, alternating between the two rows, and pull the thread up tight to pinch the bud in just below the petals.

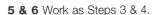

83

The following buds are green tipped with a second colour for the emerging petals. But they can also be tiny flowers if worked in the petal colour alone.

They start with Circular Peyote Stitch (worked more tightly at the centre than in the Circular Peyote Stitch Filigree Flowers) and then develop into Tubular Peyote Stitch. It is most important to remember to 'step up' at the end of each round by going through the first bead added in the round. This will ONLY be mentioned in the instructions if there is a particular difference to point out.

They are quite fiddly to work at the beginning – it helps to hold on tight to the tail of thread and support the beadwork on the top of your index finger with your thumb. Make the Large Bud first and then move on to any of the smaller buds.

SHOPPING LIST

seed beads size 11 or size 15 or cylinders in green (G) and a petal colour (P)

Large Beaker Bud
FIDDLY FACTOR

1 Pick up 6 G, run through all the beads again and the next one or two beads once more, taking care not to split the thread. Do not knot.

2 (Pick up 1G, go through the next bead) 6 times, pulling firmly to force the new beads into place.

3 (Pick up 2G, go through 1) 6 times.

4 (Pick up 1G, go through 1) 12 times.

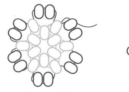

5 – 9 Repeat Step 4 five more times. The gaps between the beads will get wider as you do so, but keep pulling the thread up firmly after each addition and, by about the third repetition, you will find the work is beginning to bend over and that it is developing into a tube.

10 * Pick up 1G, go through 1; pick up 1P, go through 1; pick up 1G, go through the next 2 beads of Row 9 and pull tight (this is a decrease). Repeat from * twice. (For clarity in showing the thread path, the beads in the diagram at right have not been drawn close together as they should be in your beadwork.)

The next 4 rounds are worked straight. Pick up the beads for each round one bead at a time in the following sequence:

11 * 1P, 1P, 1G (over the decrease made in Step 10). Repeat from * twice.
12 * 1P, 1G, 1G. Repeat from * twice.
13 * 1P, 1G, 1P. Repeat from * twice.
14 all P beads. Step up at the end of the round as normal, then pass through the next bead on the edge (Row 13) and the 2nd bead added in this round.

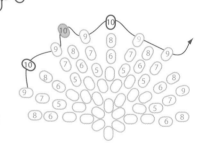

* = the 1st bead of each row

15 * (Pick up 1P, go through 1) twice. Pass down through the next bead (which was added in Step 13) and up through the next. Repeat from * twice. Step up as normal.

16 * Pick up 1P, go through 1. Pass down through the next 2 beads and up through the next 2. Repeat from * twice.

Small Beaker Bud

FIDDLY FACTOR

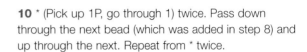

1 & 2 Work as Steps 1 & 2 of *Large Beaker Bud* but starting with 3 beads.

3 (Pick up 2G, go through 1) 3 times (6 beads added in all).

4 (Pick up 1G, go through 1; pick up 2G, go through 1) 3 times (9 beads added).

5 (Pick up 1G, go through 1) 9 times.

The next 4 rounds are worked straight, repeating Step 5. Pick up the beads for each round in the following sequence:
6 all G beads.
7 *1G, 1G, 1P. Repeat from * twice.
8 *1G, 1P, 1P. Repeat from * twice.
9 all P beads.

10 * (Pick up 1P, go through 1) twice. Pass down through the next bead (which was added in step 8) and up through the next. Repeat from * twice.

11 * Pick up 1P, go through 1. Pass through the next 4 beads along the edge. Repeat from * twice.

Winged Beaker Bud

FIDDLY FACTOR

1 – 11 Work as Steps 1-11 of *Small Beaker Bud*, but substituting this sequence of beads for Steps 7 - 9: 7. all G beads; 8. all G beads; 9. *1G, 1P, 1G. Repeat from * twice.

9A Needle through to one of the beads of Row 8 next to a P bead (of Row 9), pointing away from it. * (Pick up 2G, go through the next bead of row 8) twice. Pass through the next P and G beads. Repeat from * twice. Step up by going through the pair of beads picked up at the beginning of the row, going up through the 1st bead, then down through the 2nd and pulling on the thread so that the 2nd bead is twisted upwards.

10A * (Pick up 3G, go up through the 1st bead of the next pair and down through the 2nd. Pass through the next 3 beads of the *Basic Bud* and the next pair of beads added in Row 9. Repeat from * twice.

Tiny Beaker Bud

FIDDLY FACTOR

1, 2, & 3 Work as Steps 1, 2 & 3 of *Small Beaker Bud*.

4 (Pick up 1G, go through 1) 6 times.

The next 3 rounds are worked straight, repeating Step 4. Pick up the beads for each round in the following sequence:

    5 all G beads
    6 all P beads
    7 all P beads

8 (Pick up 3P, go through 1; pick up 1P, go through 1) 3 times (12 beads added).

Tiny Beaker Bud with Petals

FIDDLY FACTOR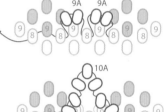

1 – 7 Using G, work as Steps 1 - 7 of *Tiny Beaker Bud*.

8 (Pick up 2P, go through 1) 6 times (12 beads added in all).

9 * pick up 3 and pass down into the next bead and up the adjacent bead. Continue around, repeating from *. (This is *Tubular Herringbone Stitch*.)

Berries

FIDDLY FACTOR

Strawberry

SHOPPING LIST

seed beads in the same shade in sizes 11 (S), 8 (M) and 6 (L), plus a few size 15 in a constrasing shade for the strawberry pips (T)

1 Pick up 1S, 2M and pass back down the S towards the tail end. Keeping hold of the tail end for tension, *pick up 1S and pass up through an M just put on (it doesn't matter which). Pick up 1M and pass down the S just put on. Repeat from* until there are 6 beads of each size.

Pass the needle down the very first M and S beneath and up through the last S and M to form the beginnings of a tube. Pass down again through the 1st M and cross the thread to the last S and then down.

Knot the beginning and end tail thread together.

2 Pass up through an S and M. * Pick up 2M, pass down the next M beneath and pass up the next M. Continue around in the same manner (in *Herringbone Stitch*), repeating from * twice. You may find it easier at this stage to work around a cocktail stick or something similar. Now reverse the direction of working and pass the needle back around the tube, not adding any beads, to straighten and reinforce the entire row. Keep the tension firm. (When you look down on the tube you should see a thread across the top of every bead.)

3 Repeat the previous row twice using the L beads, and then a final row using the S beads again. Keep the tension firm at all times and remember to check that every row has a thread across the top of every bead.

4a Now strengthen the structure by embellishing with additional S beads. With the needle exiting through the top of an L bead towards the top of the berry (Bead X) * pick up 1S and pass down the next L. Pick up 1S and pass up an L bead. Continue around from *, finishing by coming up through Bead X.

b Pass through the 1S put on at the beginning of the row, down the L (bead Y) and reverse the direction of working. Pick up 1S and pass up through the next L. Pick up 1S and continue around in the same manner. (There should be 6 small embellishing beads staggered above every large bead on the top row and 6 beneath). When finished, by coming through bead Y, pass down through the L beneath it.

c Pick up 1S and pass up through the L. Pass through the S previously put on and down the next L. Pick up 1S and continue around and then reverse the direction of working to place the rest of the beads.

5 Needle down to the bottom row of the berry, and exiting downwards * pick up 1S and pass up through the next S. Pass down the next S and continue from * around for a total of 3 new beads. Pass the thread through these new beads and pull gently and firmly.

6 Now embellish a few pips onto the berry. Needle up to the top of the berry, exiting from a L. Pass through one of the embellishing S beads just added and pick up 1T. Pass through the embellishing S immediately below it and with the needle facing in the same direction as above (so the thread path is a Z or S shape). Pass up through the next L. Continue around in the same manner and again for the row immediately below – both being rows of L beads.
Work the thread back to the beginning and knot the two ends together, and bury the ends.

Blackberry

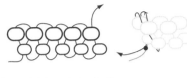

SHOPPING LIST

seed beads in the same shade in sizes 11 (S), 8 (M) and 6 (L)

1 Work as Step 1 of *Strawberry* until there are 5 beads of each size and then join end to end into a tube in the same way.

2 Pass up through an S and M. * pick up 2L and pass down the next M beneath. Pass up the next M and pick up 2L. Pass down the next M and up the last M. Pick up 1L and pass down (without picking up any more beads) into the 1st L already put on. Pass down into the M beneath and up the next M and L above.

Pass down the next L and M. Continue around the tube, not adding any beads, to straighten and reinforce the entire row. Keep the tension firm. (When you look down on the tube you should see a thread across the top of every bead.)

You may find it easier at this stage to work around a cocktail stick or something similar.

3 Repeat the previous row using M beads and then again using S beads.

4. Now strengthen the structure by embellishing with additional beads. With the needle exiting through an S bead towards the M row * pick up 1S and pass up the next S in the row. Pass down the next S and repeat from * around until all 5S beads have another S bead staggered underneath them. Pass down through the M bead below.

5 * Pick up 1S and pass the needle up through the next M, through the new linking S and down the next M. Repeat from * until all 5M beads have an S bead staggered underneath them.

6 Continue in this manner for another 2 rows, then work the thread back to the beginning and knot the two ends together, and bury the ends.

Raspberry

SHOPPING LIST

seed beads in sizes 11 and size 8 and tiny drops (DP)

all in a similar shade

1 & 2 Work as Steps 1 & 2 of *Strawberry*.

3 Repeat the process for another row using S beads.

4 Now strengthen the structure by embellishing with additional beads. With the needle exiting up through any bottom (or top) bead away from the structure *pick up 1DP and pass down through the next S and up the next. Continue from * until there are 3 beads added, and then reverse the direction of working to put the next 3DP beads on. When finished pass through to the next row and continue in the same manner over the entire bead in the same way, making a total of 5 rows of embellishing beads.

5 You will see that the two central rows of M beads look a little bald. With the needle exiting from a DP above an M row pick up 1DP and pass diagonally down through the embellishing DP in the row below. Then pick up 1DP and pass diagonally up through the embellishing DP in the row above (like a V). Continue around in the same manner.

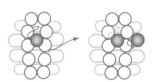

Repeat this process again for the lower row of M beads, immediately below, then work the thread back to the beginning, knot the two ends together, and bury the ends.

CALYX

LARGE CALYX

SIMPLE SEPAL

LARGE SEPAL

Sepals & Stamens FIDDLY FACTOR

Some of the flowers will look really pretty with sepals behind them to give them more emphasis (they will also work as mini leaves). You could make them individually or work them around a circle of beads as a calyx which would make them easier to add to the flowers when attaching to your project.

The stamens serve a dual purpose for our beaded flowers: they are of course necessary for the flower, but they are also in the perfect position for using as the fixing attachment of the flower to the project. Remember to make sure that the beads you choose for the stamen are big enough to fill the centre of the flower or use a larger bead as a washer underneath and possibly on top as well and then do check that they are secure by giving a little tug!

In some instances it's better to attach the stamens to the flower at the time of making – possibly because the stamens are an integral part of the concept of the flower, or they are more obvious; or because it's just plain easier. This will particularly be the case if they are long stamens with a swing such as the fuchsia. These stamens follow the same beading principles as a fringe and need the tension to be loose to allow for 'drape' or 'swing' which will not be possible if they are being used at the same time to fix the flower in position.

Simple Sepals

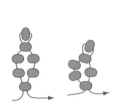

Pick up 5, pass back through 4th; pick up 2 or 1.

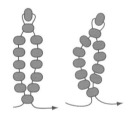

Pick up 8, pass back through 4the; pick up 5 or 4.

Pick up the beads for the length of the sepal and pass back through the penultimate bead. Pick up beads for the second side of the sepal and pass back through the 1st bead. The examples here give two lengths and also show that the sepals do not have to be symmetrical – using just one less bead on one side of the sepal than the other introduces some shaping and can make quite a difference when working on this small scale.

Calyx

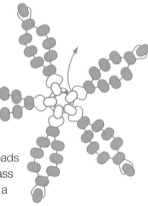

To make a group of *Simple Sepals* together as a calyx, start from a circle and work each individual sepal off it.

Pick up the same number of beads as you want to make sepals, pass through them again to turn into a circle and knot.
Pass through the 1st bead.

Make your chosen sepal and pass through the next bead on the circle. Repeat around.
If you want a larger centre, either use a larger bead size, or work as *Large Calyx*, on the next page.

Large Sepals

The sides of the sepals can
be added to for extra fullness.
The instructions here are for a
6-bead start, but you can adapt
a *Simple Sepal* of any length in
the same way.

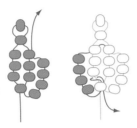

Make a *Simple Sepal* starting with 6 beads, and with 3 beads
on the second side. Turn and pick up 4 beads and pass
up through the 1st bead picked up on the second side.

Turn and go down through the adjacent bead. Pick up 4
beads and pass up the very 1st bead of the sepal. Hook
around the thread and pass back down through the 1st bead.

Large Calyx

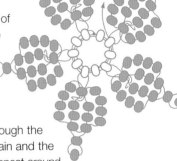

Pick up double the number of
beads as you want to make
sepals, pass through
them again to turn into
a circle and knot. Pass
through the 1st bead.

Make a Large Sepal, go through the
same bead on the circle again and the
next 2 beads on the circle. Repeat around.

Encourage the edges of the sepals to fold up, to give a lovely
3-D effect – a flower in its own right!

Simple Stamen

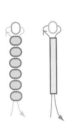

Start here with the simplest stamen of all:
pick up a few seed beads or a bulge,
add 1 bead and return through the rest.

Frilly Stamen

Pick up 5 seed beads then a drop bead. Turn,
pass through 1 seed bead and add a picot of 3
smaller beads. Pass back through the seed
bead in a circular motion and through the next
seed bead. Add another picot of any 3 smaller beads.
Continue in the same manner to the bottom of the stamen.

Branched Stamen

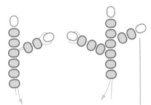

Make one *Simple Stamen* with
tiny seed beads. * Hook the
needle round a thread in the
stitching and return up through
the beads in the first stamen, exiting a few beads from
the top. Pick up 2 or 3 beads. Miss the last bead added
and go down through the rest of the beads, right down to
the base of the flower again. Repeat from * once more.

Stamen Styles

Below are several examples of bead combinations that
could be used as stamens. Some work as for *Simple
Stamen* and others as *Branched Stamen*. (And, if you
turn them upside down, they also would serve as
endings for a fringe.) Once you have made the flower
and optional calyx attach them through the centre – like
a button – with any of the following:

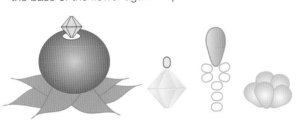

BASIC BRICK STITCH LEAF

BASIC BRICK VARIATION 1

CLOVER LEAF

BASIC BRICK
VARIATION 2

PEYOTE STITCH LEAF

TENDRIL

PEYOTE VARIATION

Leaves & Tendrils

FIDDLY FACTOR

We have kept the leaf designs very simple – to add emphasis and lushness to the flowers rather than detract from them.

Clover Leaf

1 Using green beads, work as *Simple 4-Petalled Flower* on *page 80*.

2 Pass through 5S of the 'petal'. * Pick up 6S and go through the centre 2S of the next 'petal'. Repeat from * twice, leaving a gap between the 1st and 4th 'petals'

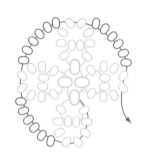

Basic Peyote Stitch Leaf

Pick up 1 small (S), 13 large (L), 1 S and go back through the 2nd bead from the needle. (Pick up 1L, miss 1, go through 1) 6 times. Go through the S from the opposite side so that the needle is pointing towards the leaf. Go on through the next two beads.

(Pick up 1, go through 1) 5 times. Turn and go down through the adjacent bead. (Pick up 1, go through 1) 5 times. ** Go through the next bead and the S at the base of the leaf and tie the two ends of thread together.

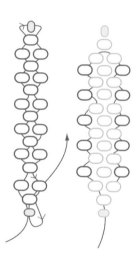

Variation

Work as *Basic Peyote Stitch Leaf* until **.

Turn and go up through the adjacent bead and the next bead.

(Pick up 1, go through 1) twice. Go up through the next bead.
Turn and go down through the adjacent bead and the next bead.
(Pick up 1, go through 1) twice.

Go through the next bead, turn and go up through the adjacent bead and the next 2 beads.

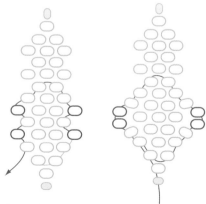

Pick up 2, go through 1 and the next 2 beads on the edge. Turn and go down through the adjacent bead and the next 2 beads. Pick up 2, go through 1 and the next 3 beads and the S at the base of the leaf.

Basic Brick Stitch Leaf

F Work as Step 1 of *Strawberry* on *page 86* using all the same size beads (B) until there are 4 beads on top and 3 below. Hook around the bottom loop and pass the needle back up so that it exits from the top of the 4th bead.

Now work in *2-drop Brick Stitch* for the next row *(see the notes on page 59)*:

1 Increase by 1 stack so that there are 5 stacks (total 10 beads)

Return to standard *Brick Stitch*:

2 - 4 Decrease by 1 bead at the beginning of each row (total 4, then 3, then 2 beads).

5 Pick up 1B and pass down the outside bead and needle down to the bottom, pulling gently to introduce a little shaping. Exit from the bottom corner bead. Finally, pick up 2B and pass into the opposite corner. If you would like more shaping then needle around the outside edge and pull gently and then return to the tail thread and knot and weave in the ends.

◆◆◆

Variation 1

F Work as the *Basic Brick Stitch Leaf*.

Now work in *2-drop Brick Stitch* for the rest of the leaf:
1 Increase by 1 stack so that there are 5 stacks (total 10 beads)

2 - 4 Decrease by 1 stack at the beginning of each row so that there are 4 stacks (total 8 beads), then 3 stacks (total 6 beads), then 2stacks (total 4 beads).

5 Pick up 1B and pass down the outside bead and needle down to the bottom, pulling gently to introduce a little shaping. Exit from the bottom corner bead. Finally, pick up 2B and pass into the opposite corner. If you would like more shaping then needle around the outside edge and pull gently and then return to the tail thread and knot and weave in the ends.

Variation 2

F Start as the *Basic Brick Stitch Leaf* until there are 5 beads on top and 4 below. Hook around the bottom loop and pass the needle back up so that it exits from the top of the 5th bead.

Now work in *2-drop Brick Stitch* for the next row:

1 Increase by 1 stack so that there are 6 stacks (total 12 beads).

Return to standard *Brick Stitch*:
2 Increase by 1 bead at the end (total 7 beads)
3 Decrease by 1 bead at the beginning (total 6 beads)
4 With the needle exiting from the top corner pass down the next bead and up the next. *Brick Stitch* for 3 beads.
5 Decrease by 1 bead at the beginning (total 2 beads)

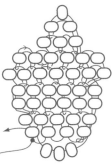

6 Pick up 1B and pass down the outside bead and needle down to the bottom, pulling gently to introduce a little shaping. Exit from the bottom corner bead. Finally, pick up 3B and pass into the opposite corner.

You might like to add a central vein: start from the centre bottom with the needle facing up towards the top point of the leaf. Pick up 5 tiny contrasting beads and pass through the central bead of the 7 bead row. Pick up 1 bead and pass back down the 5 just put on and into the next base bead on the bottom of the leaf.

If you would like more shaping then needle around the outside edge and pull gently and then return to the tail thread and knot and weave in the ends.

◆◆◆

Tendril

Pick up a line of beads alternating two sizes, beginning and ending with the smaller of the two. Work back up the line, going through the larger beads only – do not pick up any more beads as you go – taking care not to split the thread.

Pull up tight and go into the final small bead from the opposite side. Tie the two ends of thread together.

PART 4

FLOWERY BRAIDS

The simple flowery braids on the following pages all make charming

necklaces and bracelets, wearable for all occasions. But why not also use

them as edging for curtains and cushions, tie-backs and cardigans.

Or twine them around a beaded rope. Or combine them with the

flowers to make a perfectly glamorous necklace.

Flower Bud Braid

SHOPPING LIST

size 11 seed beads (S)
a mix of beads (M) for the flowerbuds – try drops,
cylinders, Magatamas, Hex beads, as well as different
sized seed beads – whatever you have in
your chosen colour scheme

FIDDLY FACTOR

1 Wrap a long length of thread around your
left index finger a few times and add 3
seed beads (S) and 5 beads (all the
same) from the mix (M). Pass the
needle back down the last 2S
towards the beginning, and then through the
1st S in the opposite direction to lock the beads in place.

2 Pass the needle back up
through the 2S.

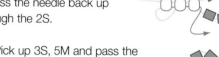

3 * Pick up 3S, 5M and pass the
needle back down the 3S just
picked up, and then through the
last M (towards the flowerbud) of
the previous group.

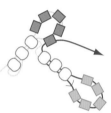

4 Repeat from * until the braid is the required length.
Vary the 5M with different beads and differing
numbers from the mix.
You may find, for example,
that 3 of the larger beads is
sufficient, rather than 5.

Variation

FIDDLY FACTOR

1 This variation uses some larger pressed flower beads as
the buds. As well as selecting your flower beads, you will
also need to add a few 3mm and/or 4mm crystals to your
mix of beads and make sure it also includes some drop beads.

2 Start the braid as above. After a few buds have been
completed, randomly replace a bud with a single flower bead.
To do this you will need to add a few additional beads to the
formula. Pick up 5S, 1 flower bead, then either: a drop bead,
or a crystal and a size 15 seed bead (T). Turn and pass back
through the crystal if used, the flower bead, 5S and then up
through the last M (towards the bud) of the previous group.

If you have a leaf (or a flower) with the hole lying horizontally
across the top instead of vertically down through the middle,
then pick up 5S, 2 or 3 T, 1 leaf, and 2 or 3 T. Pass back
down the 5S and then up through the last M (towards the
bud) of the previous group. Then pick up 3S, 3M (or 5M)
and pass the needle back down the 3S and up through
the 4th S of the previous group.

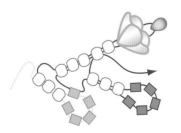

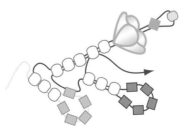

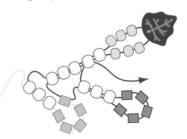

Flower Blossom Braid

SHOPPING LIST

seed beads in two sizes – the smaller is
for the stalks (S) and the flower 'petals' (P);
the larger is for the flower centres (C)

FIDDLY FACTOR

1 Wrap a length of thread (the same colour as the stalk)
around the finger of your non-dominant hand a few times,
and pick up 3 stalk-coloured beads (S), 5 flower-coloured
beads of the same size as
S (P), and 1 flower-centre
bead of a larger size (C).
Pass the needle down the
first P put on in the opposite
direction.

2 Pick up 3P and pass through
the last P of the previous
group, push the entire flower
into position above the S
beads then pass the needle (continuing
in the same direction) on through the remaining 4P beads
and 2 of the S beads, then through the 1st S in the
opposite direction to lock the beads in place.

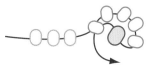

3 Pass the needle back up through
the 2S. * Pick up 3S, 5P, 1C and
pass down the 1st P in the
opposite direction.

4 Pick up 3P and pass through the last P of
the previous group. Push the flower into
position. Pass the needle
around in the same
direction through the
remaining 4P beads and
down the 3S beads.

Then pass the needle up the
2nd P bead of the previous flower
blossom (check again that the flower is in
position and without excess bare thread).

Continue repeating from * until the braid
is the desired length.

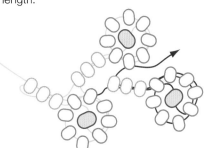

95

Leaf & Flower Blossom Braid

SHOPPING LIST

seed beads in two sizes – the smaller is
for the stalks and the flower 'petals';
the larger is for the flower centres.

FIDDLY FACTOR

1 - 4 Work as Steps 1 - 4 of *Flower Blossom Braid*.

5 When you have made 2 flowers * pick up 8S and pass
the needle back down the 7th S in the opposite direction.
Pick up 2S and pass the needle down the 4th S and
back down the first 3S just put on**.

Pass the needle up through the 2nd P bead of the previous
flower blossom and repeat from * to **. Pass the needle
up through the 3rd S bead of the previous leaf ***

Continue from * to *** until there are five leaves, two on
one side and three on the other.

Continue until the braid is the desired length,
alternating two flowers with five leaves.

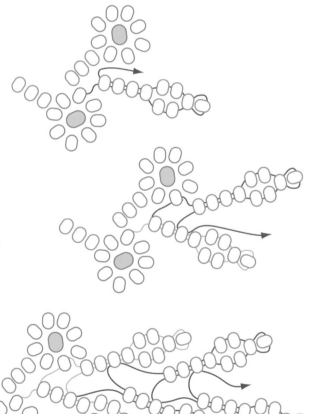

Peyote Blossom Braid

SHOPPING LIST

seed beads in one size or cylinders

FIDDLY FACTOR

1 Pick up 5 background beads (B) and go back through the 3rd bead from the needle (bead 3). Pick up 1B and go through the very first bead.

2 Pick up 1 petal bead (P) and go back through the last bead added in the previous row. Pick up 1B and go through the next bead.

3 Pick up 1B and go back through the last bead added in the previous row. Pick up 1P and go through the next bead.

4 Continue in this manner, picking up 2 beads each row and following Chart A until you have added 18 beads in total. Bead 17 will be the first P of the second flower along the braid.

5 Pick up 3P and weave through the P beads already in place.

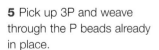

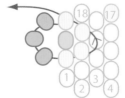

6 Work another 5 rows from Chart A, until you have added the first P bead of the third flower. Repeat Step 5.

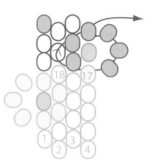

7 Continue working in *Peyote Stitch* following Chart A. The rows to repeat are indicated by the dotted lines.

Each time you add the first P bead of a flower, remember to add the 3 extra P beads on the side of the previous flower before you go on to the next row.

pattern repeat

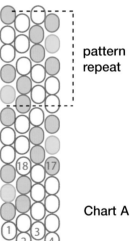

8 To finish the braid so that the end matches the beginning, work 2 rows plain after completing the final flower.

Chart A

Flowery Bead Braid

SHOPPING LIST

seed beads in one size or cylinders

a selection of pressed glass

flower beads

FIDDLY FACTOR

This braid features pressed glass flower beads and couldn't be easier or quicker to do.

1 Put a stop bead on two lengths of thread, leaving 15 cms - 20 cms (6" - 8") tails.

2 With one of the threads, * pick up 2 seed beads for the stem, 1 Flower bead and 1 seed bead for the centre of the flower and go back through the Flower bead. Repeat from *, pulling the thread through as snugly as you can with each addition. There will be small gaps with thread showing. Continue until the braid is longer than you require by about 40-50%.

3 With the second thread, pass through all the stem seed beads, pulling the gaps closed. The Flower beads will be much closer together and will sit on all sides of the braid. Adjust the length as necessary by

adding to or removing beads from the first thread, then run through the stem beads with the second thread and pull up.

4 Pick up 1 seed bead and go back into the stem and secure. Take the other thread through the same seed bead, go down into the stem and secure.

5 Remove the stop bead and finish off as in Step 4.

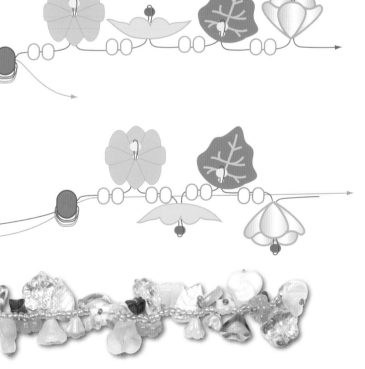

Daisy Chain

6-bead

SHOPPING LIST

seed beads in one size

FIDDLY FACTOR

1 Pick up 4 Petal beads in the first colour (P) and 1 in a contrasting colour (C).

Pass back down the first P in the opposite direction.

2 Pick up 2P and pass through the 4th P in the opposite direction. Pull tight.

3 Plck up several seed beads to give the length you want between daisies.

Repeat Steps 1, 2 and 3 until the required length is reached.

Variation: 8-bead

SHOPPING LIST

seed beads in one (or two) sizes

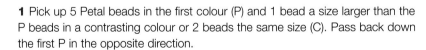

FIDDLY FACTOR

1 Pick up 5 Petal beads in the first colour (P) and 1 bead a size larger than the P beads in a contrasting colour or 2 beads the same size (C). Pass back down the first P in the opposite direction.

2 Pick up 3 P and pass through the 5th P in the opposite direction. Pull tight.

3 Plck up several seed beads to give the length you want between daisies.

Repeat Steps 1, 2 & 3 until the required length is reached.

Daisies in a Row

6-bead

FIDDLY FACTOR

SHOPPING LIST

seed beads in one size

1 & 2 Work as for *Daisy Chain*.

3 * Pick up 1 bead in a different petal colour (PP) and pass back into the last bead put on from the opposite direction.

4 Pick up another PP and pass back into the last bead just put on from the opposite direction.

5 Pick up 2PP and 1C and pass into the 2nd bead (PP) of this flower from the opposite direction.

6 Pick up 2PP and pass into the corner bead (the 4th PP of the flower) in the opposite direction.

Repeat from * until the required length is reached.

Variation: 8-bead

FIDDLY FACTOR

SHOPPING LIST

seed beads in one (or two) sizes

1 & 2 Work as for *Daisy Chain, Variation (8-bead)*.

3 * Pick up 1 bead in a different petal colour (PP) and pass back into the last bead put on from the opposite direction.

4 Pick up another PP and pass back into the last bead just put on from the opposite direction.

5 Pick up 3PP and 1large C (or 2 same size C) and pass into the 2nd bead (PP) of this flower from the opposite direction.

6 Pick up 3PP and pass into the corner bead (the 5th PP of the flower) in the opposite direction.

Repeat from * until the required length is reached.

Cosy Daisy Chain

6-bead

FIDDLY FACTOR

SHOPPING LIST

seed beads in one size

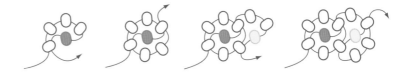

1 & 2 Work as for *Daisy Chain*.

3 * Pick up 2P and 1C and pass into the last P bead added in the last flower from the opposite direction.

4 Pick up 2P and pass into the 2nd P just added in the opposite direction.

Repeat from * until the required length is reached.

You can work this braid as an 8-bead variation if you wish, referring back to the *8-bead Variation* of *Daisy Chain* to guide you.

Variation: using Drop Beads

SHOPPING LIST

seed beads in one size
drop beads

FIDDLY FACTOR

1 Work *Cosy Daisy Chain (6-bead)* using beads all the same colour for the background (B) until you are ready to add the first Drop Bead Daisy.

2 * Pick up 1B, 1 Drop bead (D) and 1B and pass into the last B bead added from the opposite direction.

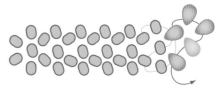

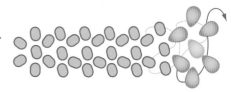

3 Pick up 1B and 1D and pass into the D just added in the opposite direction.

4 Pick up 2D and 1Drop bead of a different colour for the centre of the Daisy and pass into the D just added in the opposite direction.

5 Pick up 2D and pass into the 2nd D just added in the opposite direction. Make sure to keep the thread pulled up tightly to hold the Drop Beads in place.

6 Continue working in B until you are ready for the next Drop Bead Daisy.

Repeat from * until the required length is reached, finishing with a section of background beads.

Daisies with Leaves

SHOPPING LIST

seed beads in one (or two) sizes

FIDDLY FACTOR

1 & 2 Work as Steps 1 & 2 of *Daisy Chain, Variation (8-bead)*.

3 * Pick up 1 green bead (G), 1 Petal bead of a different colour (PP) and 1G and pass into the last P bead added in the last flower from the opposite direction.

4 Pick up 1G and 1PP and pass into the PP just added in the opposite direction.

5 Pick up 3PP and 1 large C (or 2 same size) C and pass into the PP just added from the opposite direction.

6 Pick up 3PP and pass into the 3rd PP just added in the opposite direction.

Repeat from * until the required length is reached.

Variation

FIDDLY FACTOR

In this variation, three different types of leaf in very small seed beads are added along the edges of the braid as it is worked. The three leaves to choose from are:

a Pick up 8 green small seed beads (S) and go back through the 2nd bead from the needle. Pick up 6S and go through the 2G of the braid.

b Pick up 8S, go back through the 2nd bead from the needle and the next 2 beads. Make a 'branch' by picking up 3 or 4S, miss the last bead and go back through the others. Pass through the next 2 or 3 beads of the main strand of 8S. Make another 'branch' and go through the remaining S beads and the 2G of the braid.

c Pick up 10S and go back through the 2nd bead from the needle. (Pick up 1, miss 1, go through 1) 4 times and the 2G of the braid.

SHOPPING LIST

seed beads in one (or two) sizes, plus very small beads for the leaves

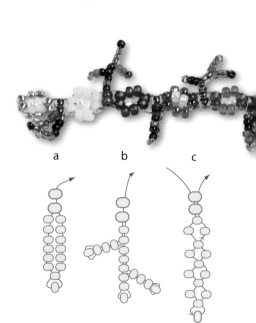

a   b   c

1 & 2 Work as for *Daisy Chain, Variation (8-bead)*.

3 * Pick up 2 green beads (G) and go through the 2P beads on the edge of the last daisy and the 2G once more.

4 Make a leaf.

5 Pick up 2PP and go through the 2G beads on the edge of the braid and the 2 PP once more.

6 Pick up 3PP and 1large (or 2 same size) C and go through the 1st of the 2PP just added. Pick up 3PP and go through the 3rd of the 3PP just added.

7 Work as Step 3.

8 Make a second leaf.

9 Work as Step 5.

10 Pick up 3PP and 1large (or 2 same size) C and go through the 1st of the 2 PP just added. Pick up 3PP and go through the 3rd of the 3 PP just added.

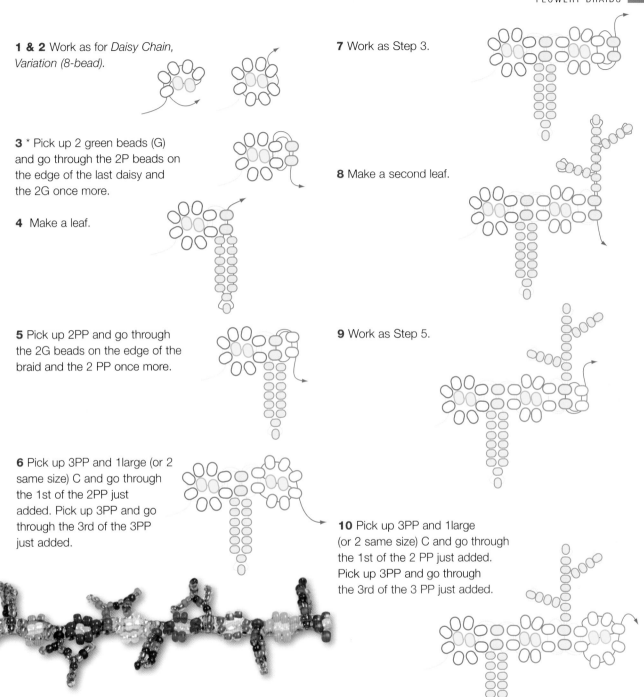

Repeat from * until the required length is reached. Vary the number of beads used for the leaves and work groups of two or three leaves of the same type rather than simply alternating them one after the other along the braid.

PART 5

THE PROJECTS

These delightful designs incorporate flowers from the Flower Collection and contain a variety of styles suitable for all abilities and tastes (and here the Fiddly Factor relates to the making of the overall project itself rather than to the braid or flower that is used for it). There is also a new flower and its project, the Anemone Corsage, which is on a larger scale; and finally, two graphs which will make lovely pictures.

Spring Confetti Brooch

SHOPPING LIST

sieve brooch

5 or 6 Daffodils with long and short trumpets (or other spring flowers)

4 long leaves *(see Brick Stitch Leaf Variation 1 on page 90)*

a few green seed beads and 3mm bugles

3 or 4 pressed glass leaves

a few 4mm bicone crystals (or larger if your daffodils are bigger than size 15)

and small bell flower beads (or similar)

Fireline or other similarly strong thread such as button thread

FIDDLY FACTOR

Prepare all the elements and gauge how they will look together. The arrangement needs to look very full, with all the flowers crammed in together, overlapping one another, and the leaves around the outside like an old-fashioned nosegay. When you are satisfied that you have prepared enough elements, stitch them in position on the sieve brooch.

1 Sew all the long leaves into position around the edge of the sieve using a strong thread.

2 Now add the flowers:

Pick up a long trumpet daffodil, a 4mm crystal, a 3mm bugle and a seed bead. * Turn and pass back down the bugle and crystal and back into the sieve. Turn and pass back up past the bicone and add another bugle and seed bead. Repeat from * until there are 3 bugles.

Pick up a short trumpet daffodil, a small bell flower bead, and seed bead. Turn and pass back down the small bell flower bead and the daffodil and into the sieve.

Repeat until all the daffodils are stitched down.

3 Place the pressed glass leaves in a ring around the perimeter, in front of the beaded leaves but behind the daffodils so that they frame the flowers. Finally fill in any gaps with a few mini leaves and sepals *(see page 88)* worked in toning beads.

Datura Earrings

This stunning little flower, reminiscent of an exotic tubular datura, makes a lovely earring. Or you could us it as a very special addition to some fringing.

SHOPPING LIST

for a pair of earrings

a small quantity of size 11 seed beads, green

a small quantity of size 15 seed beads, 2 shades of pink

a few size 15 seed beads for the stamens

6 tiny drops • earring hooks

FIDDLY FACTOR

F & 1 Use green size 11 seed beads. The Foundation and 1st Row of the *Tubular* section at the top of the earring are worked the same as F & 1 of the *Basic Herringbone Daisy Flower* on *page 12*, but starting with only 6 beads.

2 To start working in *Tubular Herringbone*, * pick up 2 and pass down into the bead below and up the adjacent bead. Continue around, repeating from * and pulling very firmly between every stitch. Step up at the end of the row. *(For more guidance on working Tubular Herringbone, see page 50).*

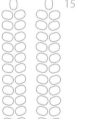

3 – 14 Change to size 15 seed beads in your first shade and work as Row 2, remembering to step up at the end of each row.

15 Place 1 bead on the top of each rib.

Add a stamen to each of the pairs of beads of Row 14, using 6, 7 or 8 beads and a tiny drop for each one.

To make the Frilly Ruffle

15A With the thread exiting one of the beads added in Row 15, * pick up 5 beads and go through the next bead added in that row. Repeat from * twice. Pass through the first 3 beads added in this row.

16A (Pick up 7 beads and go through the 3rd bead of the group of 5 beads added in the previous row) 3 times.

17A Change to the second shade of size 15 to work picots all around: go through the 1st bead of a group of 7 added in the last round. * (Pick up 3, miss 1 bead, go through the next bead) 3 times. Pick up 3, go through the 1st bead of the next group of 7. Repeat from * twice.

Return to the first shade of size 15s to make the outer frilly ruffle:

15B with the thread exiting one of the beads added in Row 15 again, * pick up 7 beads and go through the next bead added in that row. Repeat from * twice. Pass through the first 4 beads added in this row.

16B (Pick up 9 beads and go through the 4th bead of the group of 7 beads added in the previous row) 3 times. Pass through the 1st bead added in this row.

17B * (Pick up 5 beads, miss 3 and go through the next) twice. Pass through the next bead (added in Row 15B) and the first bead of the next group of 9. Repeat from * twice (but, at the end of the round, do not go into the group of 9).

18B Change to the second shade of size 15 to work picots all round: go through the 1st bead of a group of 5 added in the last round. * (Pick up 3, miss 1 bead, go through the next bead) twice. Pick up 3, go through the 1st bead of the next group of 5. Repeat from * 5 times.

Return to the tail of thread at the beginning of the *Herringbone* tube. (Pick up 1 size 11, go through 2) 3 times. Go through the 3 new beads again a few times, pulling them tightly into a circle and finish off the thread. Use a fresh thread to stitch on the earring hook.

Blossom Necklace

FIDDLY FACTOR

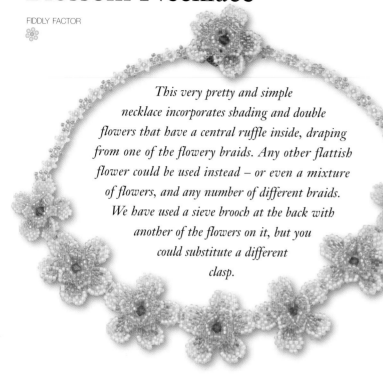

This very pretty and simple necklace incorporates shading and double flowers that have a central ruffle inside, draping from one of the flowery braids. Any other flattish flower could be used instead – or even a mixture of flowers, and any number of different braids. We have used a sieve brooch at the back with another of the flowers on it, but you could substitute a different clasp.

Make a flower in the size 11 seed beads from *Brick Stitch Variation 4* using the colour shade chart and with the Foundation Row in dark beads.

Without finishing the thread, return to the Foundation Row and add a *Netted Ruffle* as described on page 49 using the following shading:

Row 1 D

Row 2 L

Row 3 M

Row 4 D

Make another 5 flowers in these beads and then 2 flowers in the size 15 seed beads.

Lay the flowers out so that the two smaller flowers are on either end and one flower is set aside for the clasp. Rotate the flowers so that one of the five petals is facing upwards and two either side are touching their neighbours with the other two facing downwards.

Leaving a very long tail that will be used later, start with a smaller flower and needle through to exit from the top of the side petal. Pass through the top inside bead, pick up 2M and pass down the next top inside bead, then across to the other petal and up through the corresponding inside bead in that petal. Pick up 2M and pass through the next top inside bead and around into the original petal. Pass all the way around again, to exit at the top of the new petal.

Needle down the new petal to the centre of that flower and exit at the Foundation Row. Pick up a crystal and pass through into the opposite side of the Foundation Row. Needle up the appropriate petal and continue around in the same manner.

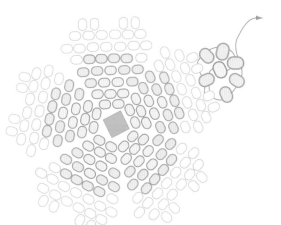

At the top of the final petal (of the small flower) pass through the top inside bead, pick up 1M (now working in size 11) and pass through the next top inside bead. Pick up 3M and 1D and pass back down the 1st M (between the smaller beads on the petal) in the opposite direction. Pass through the top inside bead of the petal and pick up 2M. Pass through the 3rd M (of the 3M just put on) in the opposite direction. Pull tight.

Now continue to make the *Daisies in a Row on page 100* from Step 3 for approximately 13 cms (5") and attach to the sieve clasp.

Return to the opposite side of the necklace and place the crystal in the appropriate position, and then make *Daisies in a Row* in the same way and attach to the clasp. Sew the final flower into position on the sieve, being careful to position the metal tongues away from the beads.

Zig Zag Lariat

SHOPPING LIST

10 - 15 g size 11 seed beads (S)

5 - 10 g cut cylinders (C)

the components for 4 Fuchsias made using size 15 seed beads,

following the instructions *on page 58*

4 x size 8 seed beads and 4 x size 6 seed beads to tone

with the lariat

FIDDLY FACTOR

The Zig Zag Braid which we have used for this lariat couldn't be easier to make. It is really a very simple variation of a basic ladder stitch. By adding in an extra bead each time you make a stitch, the strip of beadwork zig zags to left and right repeatedly. We have used a cut cylinder bead for the central ladder stitch for extra twinkle and a size 11 seed bead for the beads which sit along the outside.

Make two lengths of Zig Zag Braid, each measuring approximately 150 cms (60"):

1 Pick up 1C and 1S and go through the C once more. Pull the thread firmly so that the S sits on top of the C. Make sure to leave a long tail of thread, at least 30 cms (12"), for attaching a fuchsia later.

2 Pick up 1C, 1S and go through the previous C. Pull the thread firmly to draw the beads close together and go through the new C once more.

Repeat Step 2 and you will find that the new seed bead will sit on the opposite side of the cylinders.

Tip

A lot of thread will show, so it is very important to choose the colour carefully, either to blend in with your beads, or to show as a deliberate contrast.

Continue repeating Step 2 until the braid is as long as you require, leaving a long tail of thread at the end to attach a fuschia.

The Fuchsias & assembling the Lariat

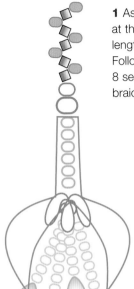

1 Assemble the fuchsias and attach them to the braid at the same time, one fuchsia at each end of of both lengths of braid.

Follow the instructions on *page 59*, placing just 1 size 8 seed bead and 1 size 6 seed bead between the braid and flower.

2 Holding both lengths of braid together, fold them roughly in the centre.

Tie an overhand knot with all four strands approximately 10 cms - 12 cms (4" - 5") above the fuchsias.

3 To wear the lariat, have the centre fold of the strands at centre front and drop the fuchsias through so that the loops sits just underneath the knot. For added security, you could instead take just two of the fuchsias and drop them through the loop so that it is held against the knot and cannot slip, as shown in the photograph.

If at any time you want to wear the lariat higher up, tie another overhand knot loosely above the first. Drop all four fuchsias and the first knot through the loop and let it settle between the knots.

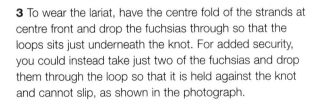

Crinkle Charm Bracelet

SHOPPING LIST

10 g size 11 seed beads, soft green (G)

8 g size 15 seed beads, pale pink (P)

8 g size 15 seed beads, strong pink (S)

25 assorted Swarovski crystals (C) (mainly 3mm and 4mm bicones / rounds, a few 6mm cushions)

6 x 5mm or 6mm Swarovski bicones for attaching the flowers

a few size 8 seed beads (12) for attaching the flowers

clasp

For the charms:

3 Pinks made following the instructions *on page 69* using beads from above (or a slightly different shade if you prefer) plus some pink size 11 seed beads

This charm bracelet in Tubular Herringbone Stitch is very easy to make and produces a very attractive slightly flattened crinkly ribbon braid. You can twist it by hand a little more when it's finished or leave it as it is.

Any charm(s) could then be used on the bracelet. This one has pinks, but it could just as easily be a berry or a columbine or a fuchsia, or any combination. There are three flowers, again you could add more.

FIDDLY FACTOR

The Bracelet

1 Foundation

Pick up 3G and pass back down the 1st G, but in the opposite direction (towards the tail). Leave a long tail that can be used to attach the clasp later and knot the two threads together. Pick up 1G and pass up through 1 of the beads above (it doesn't matter which). Pick up another G and pass down through the 4th G (the bead just added). Continue in this zig zag manner until there are 8 beads in total – 4 on top and 4 below.

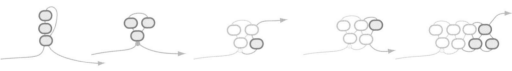

Sew the beginning and end stacks together to form a tube. (Pass the needle down the very 1st 2 beads and pull gently until the two ends meet, and then pass the needle up the very last 2 beads. Pass back down the 1st 2 beads and then knot the threads together and pass the thread back up to the top row.)

2 Tubular Herringbone Stitch

With your needle exiting any of the beads on top of the tube pick up 2G and pass down the next bead on the tube. Pass up the next bead and pick up 2G and pass down the next bead on the tube. Pass up the next bead on the tube and on up the new bead added in this row – this is the step up and will complete 1 row.

Now start adding the tiny beads: pick up 1G, 1P and pass down the next bead on the tube. Pass up the next bead and pick up 1G, 1S and pass down the next bead on the tube. Step up and continue in this same manner until the bracelet is the required length (about 7") allowing for the clasp. Finish off the last 3 rows using G beads only to match the beginning. Needle around the last row to join it all together.

3 Attach the clasp to either end.

To embellish the Bracelet and add the charms

The bracelet has 4 lines of beads running along its length: two of the G beads and one each of the P and S. *(Note – the lines of beads are shown straight in the diagram below, but yours will be twisting because of the varying sizes of beads.)*

Working on the line of tiny P beads first, add picots all the way along: pass through the 1st P bead, pick up 3P and pass through the 3rd P bead on the rib. Continue along in the same manner, picking up 3P, missing a bead on the line and passing through the next bead.

Embellish all four lines of beads in the same manner, using the appropriate bead for each line.

Then work on the strong pink line of tiny seed beads to add the charms and crystals: starting from the centre bead of the very 1st picot, pick up 1G, a 6mm bicone, a flower, 4 x size 8 seed beads, a 6mm bicone, and 1S.

Turn and pass back through the bicone, the size 8 beads, flower, bicone, and 1G (tugging gently to make sure that all is secure); and along the rib of S beads, bypassing the next picot * and then up the next picot to exit from the centre bead.

Pick up 1S, a crystal (any), and 1S. Turn and pass back down the crystal and the 1S and back through the centre bead of the picot and the last bead of the picot. Pass along the line of S beads, bypassing the next picot and continue from * adding a crystal on every other picot until you reach the centre point of the bracelet.

Add a flower instead of a crystal and continue in the same manner as before, adding another flower at the very end.

Rosette Pendant

This versatile jewellery combination gives you two styles of necklace and/or a brooch. We have worked in blues and greens to match the cornflower on the pendant. But you can choose any of the flowers to stitch to the pendant, for example a water lily or peony, and adapt your colour scheme to suit.

FIDDLY FACTOR

The Necklace

1 Refer to the instructions for *Leaf & Blossom Braid* on *page 96* and make a braid as long as you want for the necklace, allowing approximately 3 cms (1") for the fastening. Mix your green beads together and pick them up randomly as you stitch. Use one shade of blue for each blossom, varying the shades along the length of the braid. Use the cream beads for the centre of each blossom.

2 For the Flower Button, make a *Basic Circular Peyote Stitch Flower (see page 44)*. Work a tube in *Peyote Stitch* off the circle for 3 or 4 rounds *(see page 53)*. Run the thread through the 4 beads of the last round a few times to pull the end of the tube tightly together into a circle.

To make the shank, with the thread coming out of one of the beads of the circle, pick up 5 green beads and stitch into the next bead but one. Pass back through the green beads and into the original circle bead, but from the opposite side. Follow the thread path again to reinforce the shank. Attach the Flower Button to one end of the braid.

3 Add a loop of beads to the other end of the braid through which the Flower Button will fit snugly, passing through it several times for strength.

SHOPPING LIST

For the Necklace:

a selection of size 11 seed beads in 4 or 5 shades of each of green and blue,

approx 25 - 30 g total • 5 g size 8 seed beads, cream

clasp (optional) or bead a fastening following the instructions given above

For the Pendant:

a Cornflower made using size 11 seed beads, following the instructions *on page 62*

size 11 seed beads in green for the circular background, approx 10 - 15 g

50 x size 8 seed beads, green • a few pressed glass flower beads

brooch back (optional)

The Pendant

Circular background

1 – 4 Use green size 11 seed beads. Work as for *Basic Circular Peyote Stitch Flower* Steps 1 - 4.

5 Pick up 1, go through 1; repeat this right around the edge of the circle, remembering to step up at the end of the round.

6 & 7 Work as Row 5.

8 * (Pick up 1, go through 1) 3 times. Pick up 2, go through 1.
** Repeat from * to ** 4 times (20 beads)

8 * (Pick up 1, go through 1) 3 times. Pick up 2, go through 1. **
Repeat from * to ** 4 times (20 beads).

9 Work as Row 5.

10 Repeat from * to ** 5 times (25 beads).

11, 12, & 13 Work as Row 5, changing to size 8
seed beads for Rows 12 & 13.

14 Switch to size 11 seed beads. ** (Pick up 1,
go through 1) 4 times. Pick up 2, go through 1.
*** Repeat from ** to *** 5 times (30 beads)

15 Work as Row 5.

16 (Pick up 3, go through 1.
Pick up 1, go through 1) 15 times.

Cornflower

Stitch the cornflower to the centre of the rosette.

Fringes

Make a length of *Flowery Bead Braid (see page 98)* and two lengths of *Leaf and Flower Blossom Braid*
– ours were between 5 cms and 10 cms (2" and 4") long. Attach them to the back of the rosette,
a little above the bottom edge.

Hanging loop

Leaving a long tail of thread at the start, make a strip of peyote stitch 4 beads wide by
8 -10 rows long:

Rows 1 & 2 Pick up 4 beads. Pointing towards the tail of thread, * pick
up 1 bead, miss a bead, go through the next bead. Repeat from * once.

Rows 3 * Pick up a bead, go through the next 'up' bead. Repeat from once.

Repeat Row 3 backwards and forwards until the strip is the length you need.

Use the tail of thread to attach the first row of the strip to the rosette along Rows 15 and 16.
Attach the other end of the strip to the rosette so that the strip lies quite flat against it,
but making sure that there is room for the necklace to slide through. You may find that you
need to adjust the number of rows in the strip depending upon your beads and tension.

To wear

You can wear the necklace on its own or thread it through the hanging loop at the back of the pendant.
If you wish to use the pendant as a brooch, thread a brooch back through the hanging loop.

Bramble Cuff

This highly decorative cuff bracelet is made in simple stages, adding as much embellishment as you choose. The main stitches are Brick for the base of the cuff and the leaves; and Herringbone, which is used to create the delicate flowers and the blackberries.

FIDDLY FACTOR

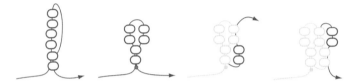

SHOPPING LIST

For the bracelet base:

20 g seed bead size 11 main colour M

10 g seed bead size 11 softer colour S

10 g seed bead size 11 contrast colour C

8 g seed bead size 15 toning colour T

8 g small drop beads DP • wide clasp

For the leaves:

a few cylinders in two shades

For the calyx and additional embellishment of the bracelet:

8 g seed bead size 15 contrasting colour TC

For the baby blossoms:

a few seed bead size 15 in three shades

6 Blackberries in a toning shade made following the instructions *on page 87*

Cuff Bracelet

For the Foundation Row: pick up 6M and pass back down the first 2 put on in the opposite direction. Knot the two threads together. Pick up 2M and pass up through 2 of the beads above (either pair, it doesn't matter which). Pick up another 2M and pass down the 2 beads just put on.

Continue in the same manner until there are about 80 stacks of beads (40 on top and 40 on bottom, 160 beads in total). Check the length for your wrist, allowing for the clasp and adjust accordingly.

Now work in *2-drop Brick Stitch* (each row is worked the same): pick up 4 beads and pass the needle under the thread joining the top of the beads in the previous row and back up through the 3rd and 4th beads. Pull gently so that the 4 beads sit correctly. Pick up 2 beads and pass the needle under the next loop and back up through both new beads. Repeat from * until you have used all the loops of thread of the previous row.

Make a further 3 rows in this colour then change to S and make 2 rows. Add a further 2 rows in S to the other side of the Foundation Row.

To make the main thorny fringe start at one outside corner and * pick up 3T, 1C, 1T, 1DP, and 1T. Pass the needle back down the 1C and the 3T and through the 2S in the bracelet base. Pick up 1T, 1S, 1T and pass over the top of the next double row of S towards the centre of the bracelet and into the pair of M immediately beneath.

Pass up the adjacent pair of M, pick up 1T, 1S and 1T and pass over the double row of S and into the 2S at the top of the bracelet. Pick up 6T, turn and pass back down through the 5th bead. Pick up 3T and pass back down through the 1st bead and through the 2S in the bracelet base. Pass up the next pair of S and repeat from *, alternating the fringe with the two styles and repeat all along the two long sides.

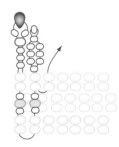

There is an additional small upper fringe which is randomly placed along the edge of the ridge just made. This includes a selection of thorny shapes and occasional individual sepals, all on a small scale, taken from the *Sepals & Stamens* on *page 88*.

Baby blossoms – make eight

Using size 15 seed beads, follow the instructions for Rows F and 1 from the *Basic Circular Herringbone Flower* on *page 12*.

2 * Pick up 4 and pass down into the 2nd new bead of the previous row. Pick up 1 (X) and pass up into the next rib. Continue around, repeating from *. Step up.

3 * Pick up 2 beads and go back up through the 2 beads on the side of the rib in a circular motion. Place 3 beads on the top of the rib, going down through both of the beads added on this side of the rib in the previous row. Pick up 2 beads and go down through both side beads again. Continue down to the bottom of the rib, across through Bead X and up to the top of the next rib. Repeat from * around the flower.

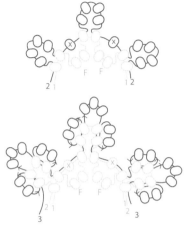

Now work back to the Foundation Row. You will see that each pair of the foundation beads has a Bead (X) sitting above it between the petals of the flower. Pass through a pair of foundation beads, pick up 1 and pass through the Bead X above it, pick up another 1 and pass in a circular motion through the pair of beads again.
Pass on to the next pair of foundation beads and repeat right round the flower.

Knot and weave in ends.

Leaves

Make 3 leaves as *Brick Stitch Leaf Variation 2* in the *Leaves and Tendrils* on *page 90*, but do not cut the thread between each leaf (so that all 3 are joined together at the base). Pass the needle around the base of all the leaves and knot and weave in ends. Make three more groups of leaves.

Calyx

Make calyx for all the blackberries following the instructions in the *Sepals and Stamens* on *page 88*.

Assembly

Arrange the blossoms, berries and leaves on the bracelet in a pleasing manner, and draw a template so that you will remember where to place them. Put some of the leaves and blossoms close to the clasp (but take care not to obstruct the fastening mechanism). Bunch the leaves up against the berries to create a more textural effect.

Sew the leaves into place first using a DP as a centre fastener.

To attach the berries, pick up 4TC, 1S, the sepal, then the berry and 1 berry-coloured seed bead. Turn and pass back down the berry and back through the other components and into the bracelet. You may like to add a few little additional thorny bits onto the bracelet in TC to create a lush affect.

Lastly attach the blossoms. Pick up 1S, the blossom, and then 1DP and pass back down into the bracelet.

Ribbon Lariat

SHOPPING LIST

15 - 20 g cylinders, background colour • 10 g cylinders for the vine pattern

20 - 25 g size 15 seed beads for the edging

5 g size 15 sead beads to match the vine

a selection of cylinders and size 15 seed beads for the flower patterns in the ribbon

12 Orchids following the instructions *on page 74*

FIDDLY FACTOR

1 Make a beaded ribbon of *Peyote Stitch*

The ribbon which forms the length of the lariat is a strip of *Peyote Stitch*. Follow Chart A to make the flowers at the beginning of the lariat and the leafy section where this end of the lariat will cross over the other. Start at the arrow where you will find directions how to start the *Peyote Stitch* ribbon, including which beads to pick up for the first four rows. You will pick up 8 beads to form Rows 1 & 2; thereafter you add 4 beads each row. (Ignore the beads labelled 'a', 'b' and 'c' for the time being.) This section of the ribbon measures 14 - 15 cms.

Continue the ribbon by following Chart B. This gives one complete pattern repeat of flowers spaced along the vine. Work as many pattern repeats as you need to give the length you require for the middle section of the lariat. Each pattern repeat measures 12 cms. Finish the section by working the flower given in Chart C.

If you find that you want to adjust the length by less than a full pattern repeat, work Chart B to the row marked **** and stop there. Turn the work over and you will be able to continue with the flower at Chart C.

Finally add the leafy section at the other end of the ribbon: follow Chart A again, but this time start at the top of the chart and work down towards the flowers at the end of the ribbon. After the final complete row, add the 3 beads marked 'a', then the 2 beads marked 'b' and then bead 'c', weaving through the work as you do so to give a shaped end to the ribbon (as illustrated in Chart D). Return to the beginning of the ribbon and add the extra beads there in the same way.

Start Chart A here and work in *Peyote Stitch*.
Rows 1 & 2: Pick up 8 beads: 1 Background (B), 3 Vine (V), 4 B.

Row 3: * Pick up 1 bead, miss a bead, go through the next bead. (Fig 1) Repeat from * 3 times. The beads to pick up are 1B, 1Flower (F), 2B. (Fig 2)

Row 4: * Pick up a bead, go through the next 'up' bead. Repeat from * 3 times. The beads to pick up are 1B, 1V, 2F (Fig 3)

Fig 1

Fig 2

Fig 3

Chart C

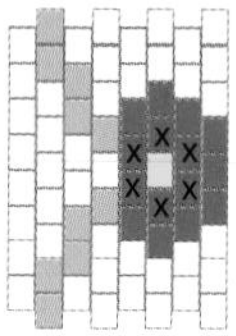

Start Chart C here ←

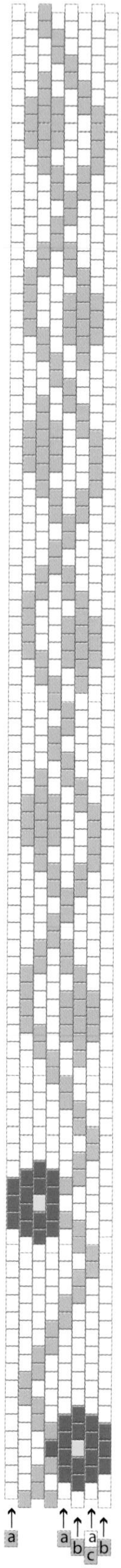

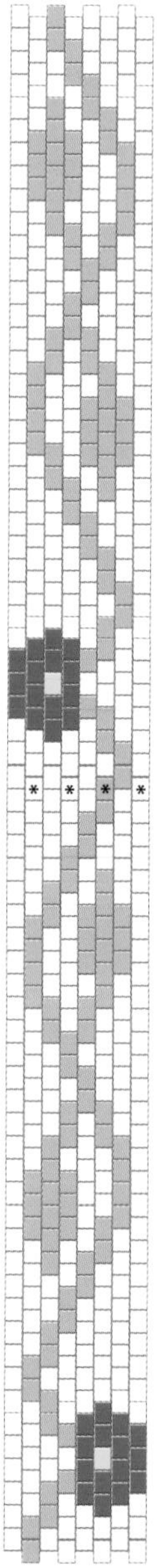

Start Chart B here ←

Chart A

Chart B

2 Embellish some flowers

Embellish the surface of the four flowers nearest to each end of the ribbon. They are described as Flowers 1, 2, 3 & 4 and are progressively complex, with Flower 4 being the orchid right at the very end of the ribbon.

Flower 1

1 Stitch 1 bead, *Square Stitch* style, on to each of the 6 red beads marked X on Chart C. (You may feel tempted to join them together into a circle – do not!) Bring the needle through one of the surface beads.

2 * Pick up 1 bead and go through the next surface bead. Repeat from * five times. At the end of the round, go through the 1st bead picked up in this round, (ie 'step up'). The new beads should sit flat against the ribbon, spreading out from the centre of the flower.
Now continue in *Circular Peyote Stitch*.

3 (Pick up 2, go through 1) six times. Step up at the end of the round.

4 * Pick up 1 size 15 bead, go through the next bead. Repeat from * eleven times.

5 (Optional) Weave back to the centre of the flower and take the needle through to the other side of the ribbon. Work Steps 1-4 again so that you have embellished both sides of the ribbon.

Flower 2

1 & 2 As for 1 & 2 of Flower 1

3 (Pick up 2, go through 1) six times. Step up at the end of the round.

4 (Pick up 1, go through 1) twelve times. Step up at the end of the round.

5 * Pick up 3 size 15 beads, go through the next bead. Repeat from * eleven times.

6 Repeat Row 5, stitching through the same beads a second time.

Flower 3

1 & 2 As for 1 & 2 of Flower 1

3 & 4 (Pick up 1, go through 1) six times. Step up at the end of the round.

5, 6, 7, & 8 As for 3, 4, 5 & 6 of Flower 2

Flower 4 – Orchid

1 Stitch five pairs of beads to the surface, following the thread path as shown in Chart D. It doesn't matter where you start from – just add a pair of beads at each arrow as you go round.

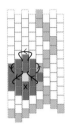

2 Following the *Orchid* instructions on *page 74*, work an upper petal on to each pair of beads. As you finish each petal, weave through the beads of the ribbon to get to the next pair of beads.

Chart D

3 For the lower petal, attach the base of 4 beads to the bead marked X in Chart D. Continue as given in the *Orchid* instructions.

3 Embellish some leaves

To embellish the 'vine' at each end of the lariat, stitch size 15 seed beads on to the surface of the leaves in the 'crossover' section of the ribbon (which you worked from Chart B) and the next two leaves.

Follow the arrows in the diagram on the unbroken line first, then the dotted line. Finally, bring the needle out on the other side of the ribbon and repeat the surface embellishment.

Note: we substituted a faceted bead for the seed bead in the very centre of the embellishment on the two leaves nearest the end of the lariat.

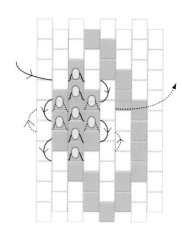

4 Edging

The edging is worked entirely in size 15 seed beads. It consists of two interlinked rows of *Brick Stitch* loops stitched on to the threads along the edge of the ribbon.

Row A

1 Bring the thread out of the edge bead at the end of the lariat. Pick up 8 beads and go under the 4th loop from the thread. Go up through the last bead picked up.

2 * Pick up 7 beads, go under the 4th loop and up through the last bead picked up. Repeat from * all along the edge.

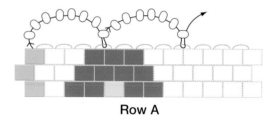

Row A

Row B

Return to the beginning of Row A, join in a new thread and bring it out through the 3rd bead along the edge in front of Row A.

1 Pick up 9 beads, take the needle behind Row A and go under the 4th loop from the thread. Go up through the last bead picked up, bringing the needle out in front of Row A.

2 * Pick up 8 beads, take the needle behind Row A, go under the 4th loop and up through the last bead picked up, bringing the needle out in front of Row A. Repeat from * all along the edge.

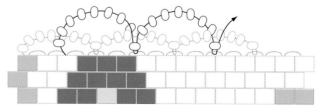

Row B

5 The Orchid Fringes

Exit Bead X in the diagram. Pick up alternating faceted beads and cylinders (C) to the length required for the first fringe.

* Pass the needle behind the threads connecting the beads at the bottom of the centre rear petal of an orchid, from the top downwards. Pick up a faceted bead and go through the hole in the centre of the circle of beads. Pick up 1C, go back through the circle of beads (the cylinder will serve as an anchor) and the faceted bead. **

Pass up through the fringe beads to the position you want to attach the next orchid. Pick up 1C, then repeat from * to **. Go through the cylinder then continue up the fringe beads and add the third orchid in the same way.

Pass up to the top of the fringe and into Bead Y. Work through the edge of the ribbon to exit Bead Z.

Work a second fringe, slightly longer than the first and placing the orchids so that they are staggered against the orchids of the first fringe.

Aerial Roots: work down each fringe again, adding 3-5 'aerial roots' on each fringe by following the instructions for the *Tendril* on *page 91*. For each aerial root, thread up approximately 5 cms of cylinders and size 15 seed beads.

Ideas for Variations

1 Keep the ribbon simple, with no 3-D embellishment. Add a simple fringe of foliage to finish.

2 Try out different colourways – *see our examples*.

3 Try a different edging.

4 Use different flowers for the fringes, for example, columbines and cornflowers for summer; tulips, daffodils and snowdrops for spring.

Anemone Corsage

FIDDLY FACTOR

❀ ❀ ❀ ❀

This fabulous brooch offers you the opportunity to make a flower on an entirely different scale from the others in the book. The more variety of shade you use in your anemone, the more realistic the effect. But if you prefer, you can use just one shade for each block of colour and it will still be very dramatic and eye-catching.

Petals

The petals of the Anemone are worked in *Square Stitch*, with minimal shaping so that you can concentrate on following the pattern charts. The petals are entirely separate from the rest of the flower, so you can make a second set in a different colour and use them interchangeably to suit your outfit and mood.

First mix together the beads for the three different areas of the petals: dark, light and white. Keep a note of the proportions of the different shades you have mixed together, like a recipe, so that you can recreate it if your stash runs low. Pick up beads for each colour block randomly from the appropriate mix of beads as you stitch.

Make 8 petals in *Square Stitch* following the charts. Each chart is different to ensure that the flower has as natural look as possible, but don't worry if the odd bead goes awry – it won't affect the overall appearance of the finished anemone. Keep the four petals on the top row of the charts separate from the slightly smaller petals of the lower row of charts.

SHOPPING LIST

For the petals:

size 15 seed beads in 3 or 4 shades of your main colour, 10 g total

a few size 15 seed beads in 2 shades of a lighter hue than your main colour

a small quantity of size 15 seed beads in white (preferably both shiny and matt)

beading thread in the finest size you can obtain, eg Nymo size O. Use a dark thread for the dark top part of the petal and a lighter shade or white for the lower part.

For the foliage:

cylinders in several shades of green (we used seven), approximately 15-20 g total

beading thread in a standard size in a dark green

For the flower centre:

a small quantity of size 15 seed beads in black (again, preferably both shiny and matt)

a few size 11 Triangles in black or very dark blue (Toho preferably for their sharp shape)

a piece of black Ultrasuede, fine leather, felt or other non-raying fabric, approx. 5 cm x 5 cm (2" x 2")

one 10p and one 5p coin (US equivalents 25c and 10c)

fine black craft wire, approx 0.3 mm diameter (28 gauge)

a little padding material, eg quilter's wadding or knitting wool

brooch back

For each petal, start at the widest row:

1 Put on a stop bead at least 15 cm (6") from the end of the thread, being careful not to split it. Thread the beads required for the widest row (the illustration here has only 8 beads across). Work across all of the beads in *Square Stitch* as described on *page 28*.

2 Remove the stop bead. Reinforce the beadwork by going straight through the beads of both rows again.

Work up towards the top of the petal and then return to the beginning to make the lower rows. Do not work the reinforcement (Step 2) on the lowest three rows of the petal. Work all the decreases as described in *Square Stitch Cupped Flowers* on *page 29*. For advice on working *Square Stitch* on a larger scale, refer to the *Tip* on *page 126*.

Having completed the chart for a petal, to give it a slightly cupped shape, weave back to the 7th or 8th Row from the bottom. Bring the needle out near the centre, pointing to the centre, pick up 1 or 2 beads of the appropriate colour and stitch into the work on the same row but 3 or 4 beads away. Pull the thread up as tight as you can and fasten off.

Arrange the petals into a circle, alternating the four slightly larger petals *(top row of the charts)* with the four slightly smaller petals *(bottom row)*. Connect the petals together by stitching through the lowest row of all eight

petals, pulling the petals closely together. Weave up into the 2nd Row and pass the needle through all the petals' second rows. Weave up into the 3rd Row. On this round, pass through all the beads of the small petals but omit the beads on each edge of the larger petals, making sure that the smaller petals sit on top of the larger ones. Pull everything up really tight and reinforce the stitching if there is enough room in the beads for more thread.

Set the petals to one side while you work on the Flower Centre.

Flower Centre

Take the piece of Ultrasuede or similar and fold it corner to opposite corner to make a triangle. Place the 10p coin on the fabric and cut around it so that you now have two circles. Set one of the circles to one side for the foliage.

Take the other circle of fabric, place the 5p coin on it centrally and draw around it. Work 4 or 5 tiny 'fringes' in the very centre of the circle using black size 15 seed beads: attach your thread securely to the fabric, pick up 3 or 4 beads, miss 1 bead and go back down through the others and into the fabric; bring the thread back through to the front of the fabric. Keep the tension tight so that each fringe stands up stiffly and work them as closely together as you can – you are aiming to obscure the fabric completely. Now work around making more fringes using only 3 beads each. Then work one more round of 2 beads per fringe, again packing them really tightly together and working to just inside the drawn line.

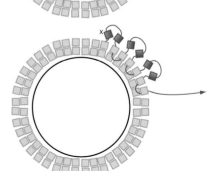

Now work around the edge of the beaded centrepiece to make the stamens. Take a piece of wire approximately 60 cms (24") long and push it through the fabric on the drawn line by the very edge of your beadwork, retaining about 2 cms (1") at the back – you may need to poke a hole through the fabric first with a strong needle if the wire itself is too bendy. Thread on 1 Triangle and hold it on the wire about 1 cm (½") above the fabric. Push the end of the wire back down through the same hole in the fabric and twist the doubled wires firmly together beneath the bead. Bring the wire back through the fabric a little way away on the drawn line at the edge of the beadwork. Continue making stamens ranging in height from 0.5 to 1 cm (¼ " to ½ ") around the centrepiece, some 25 -30 stamens in all, adding in new lengths of wire as necessary.

Set the flower centre to one side with the petals while you work on the foliage.

Foliage

The foliage has a round of *2-drop Brick Stitch* right at the centre and then a couple of rounds of *Circular Herringbone*, just like the *Herringbone Stitch Daisy Flowers*, so it is easy to get started. The leaves then separate and are worked in sections in a free way with lots of splits and spiky edges – we have given you a template to guide you but not bead by bead instructions.

Take the second circle of fabric and work in *Brick Stitch* right around the edge of it, placing a stack of two beads from the green cylinder mix with each stitch. (*See the notes on working 2-drop Brick Stitch on page 59*). At the end of the round, make sure you have an even number of stacks (there should be between 40 and 50) and complete the circle of *Brick Stitch* by going down through the very first stack and up through the last.

Now start working in *Circular Herringbone Stitch*: * pick up 2 beads and go down through the next bead along. Bring the needle up through the next bead. Repeat from * around the circle. At the end of the round, put the needle up through the very first bead picked up in the round (*marked x*), thus 'stepping up' to be ready for the following round.

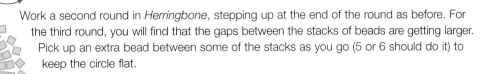

Work a second round in *Herringbone*, stepping up at the end of the round as before. For the third round, you will find that the gaps between the stacks of beads are getting larger. Pick up an extra bead between some of the stacks as you go (5 or 6 should do it) to keep the circle flat.

Now refer to the foliage template and the shaping instructions below and start to work one section at a time, splitting the circle of *Herringbone* by turning and working back along the previous row. Increase where required to keep the beadwork full and split the foliage where indicated by the template. Narrow the leaves towards their points by decreasing, again with reference to the template. To achieve a frilly, cut effect, work some 2-bead spikes especially on the edges of the leaves by repeatedly adding pairs of beads on the same spot. Lay the petals over the top from time to time to check how they look and adjust the foliage to suit (don't feel you have to follow the template exactly – it's really just a guide to get you started. If you do decide to work directly from the template, enlarging it on a photocopier by 10% will make it life-size.).

To turn at the end of a row: take the needle around the thread underneath the last bead to anchor it before going up through the edge beads *(see diagram at right)*.

To increase: pick up an extra bead between two stacks on one row, then 2 beads on the next time past, then stitch a pair of beads into them to create a new herringbone stack on the next row.

To decrease in mid-row: pick up 1 bead instead of 2 on one row; miss it on the next.

To decrease on the edge: at the beginning of a row, weave to the second pair of beads; at the end of a row, just turn before you get to the edge.

Assembling the Brooch

Stitch the brooch back to the back of the foliage. Place the 5p coin on the front of the fabric centre of the foliage, add a little padding material and then stitch the circle of fabric of the flower centre on top, back stitching neatly around the edges of the two fabric circles.

Gather the stamens together over the middle of the flower centre and lower the petals over the top. Spread the stamens out so that the petals are held in place.

A note on size: Although we have described this flower as an anemone, to be botanically accurate it should have twelve petals rather than eight. If you decide to do this, repeat two of the petals from each row of the charts and adjust the size of the flower centre to fit.

Garden Path Vista

*This evocative picture of a garden at the height of summer would make a
delightful box lid, or cushion centre. It could also be used in the centre of
a journal – of garden notes perhaps, or happy memories?*

*Once you have completed the picture, consider adding some tiny flowers
and leaves for texture on its surface, selecting from those in the Buds and
Greenery section of the book starting on page 78.*

SHOPPING LIST

a small quantity of cylinder beads in each of the
18 colours listed in the Key (*see the Tip on colour
on page 128*)
The finished weight of the picture is 22g

FIDDLY FACTOR

Design by Claire Crouchley

The picture has been made in *Square Stitch* (though you could use a
beadweaving loom if you prefer). Cylinder beads have been used because
their cylindrical shape means they fit together evenly, matching the straight
sides of a 'grid'. It is 84 beads wide x 51 rows tall and measures 12.5 cms
x 8.5 cms (5" x 3.3").

To start the picture, put on a stop bead and pick up the beads for Row 1,
going from the right to the left of the chart.

Then add the beads for Row 2, working from left to right in *Square Stitch*
(*as described on page 28*). Remove the stop bead and reinforce the
beadwork by going straight through the beads of both rows again.
(*Refer to the diagrams on page 122 to see the thread path.*)

Continue working in *Square Stitch* backwards and forwards across the chart.

We have turned the chart sideways to make it as large as possible on the
page for ease of working.

Each row of the chart is numbered to help you keep your place. However,
if you find it difficult to keep track of where you are on the chart, you might
like to take a photocopy of it and strike through a row once you have
completed it.

Square Stitch Tip

All beads, and especially very shiny
ones, for example those with a metallic
finish or a silver lining, can look very
different when viewed from different
angles because they reflect the light
differently. It is very important, when
working a large-scale project in
Square Stitch, to understand that it has
a 'nap or 'pile' like a velvet fabric
because the beads do not, as you might
expect, sit square next to each other.
Rather they are at a slight angle, and
row upon row of beads all tilting in
one direction will reflect the light in a
particular way. If you inadvertently
change the direction you are working
half way through your piece, it will
show as a marked change of colour
along a straight line.

So please be careful and remember
that your picture has a back and a
front. As long as you always pick it up
with the front towards you, you will
avoid any problems. (This matters
much less when working on a smaller
scale and is not something to consider
when making the *Square Stitch Cupped
Flowers*, for example.)

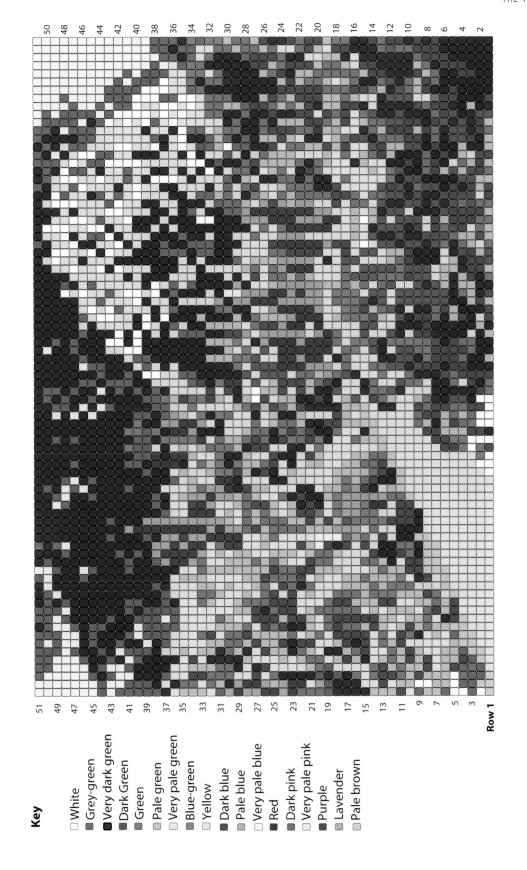

Key

- ☐ White
- ■ Grey-green
- ■ Very dark green
- ■ Dark Green
- ■ Green
- ■ Pale green
- ☐ Very pale green
- ■ Blue-green
- ☐ Yellow
- ■ Dark blue
- ■ Pale blue
- ☐ Very pale blue
- ■ Red
- ■ Dark pink
- ☐ Very pale pink
- ■ Purple
- ■ Lavender
- ☐ Pale brown

Full Bloom Picture

This glorious picture of flowers in full bloom (actually tulips) with exquisite shading from deep rich colours in their centres to gentle pinks at the edges of the petals would make a wonderful focal point on a bag, or a box lid, but it would be equally lovely in a picture frame, especially if you add to it some flowers from the Collection. Or you could create an entire frame of flowers and foliage, to make it even more special.

SHOPPING LIST

a small quantity of cylinder beads in 2 or 3 shades for each of the 14 colour blocks listed in the Key – *see the notes below*
(The finished weight of the picture is 31g)

FIDDLY FACTOR

Design by Claire Crouchley

Colour Tip

As you work, watch out for unexpected consequences when placing different colours and finishes side by side – beads with a metallic finish, for example, might appear to blend well with those around them on your beading mat, but if over-used can dominate a piece and detract from the beauty of the other beads. And the colour of one bead will influence the colour of its neighbours, as will the colour of the thread you use. If in any doubt about using a particular bead, or what colour thread to choose, work a little sample of the pattern first to check how it looks. Also, it is difficult to see the overall pattern while it is very close to you, so stand back from your work from time to time and take a look from a distance – it will snap into focus like an impressionist painting and any beads that don't quite 'work' will sing out to you.

For each of the colour blocks listed in the Key, 2 or 3 shades have been mixed together and then picked up randomly. This adds greatly to the subtlety and complexity of the design but with little extra effort in the stitching (and is a technique we also used in the petals of the *Anemone* on *page 122*). Do not worry if your bead collection is not large enough to arrive at such a mix, as working in simple blocks of colour will still give you a beautiful result.

The picture is 97 beads wide by 63 rows tall and measures 14 cms x 11 cms (5.5" x 4.3") and can be made in *Square Stitch* following the advice and instructions given for the *Garden Path Vista* on *page 126* (though you could use a beadweaving loom if you prefer – our sample has been made in this way).

We have turned the chart sideways to make it as large as possible on the page for ease of working.

Each row of the chart is numbered to help you keep your place. However, if you find it difficult to keep track of where you are on the chart, you might like to take a photocopy of it and strike through a row once you have completed it.

62 60 58 56 54 52 50 48 46 44 42 40 38 36 34 32 30 28 26 24 22 20 18 16 14 12 10 8 6 4 2

63 61 59 57 55 53 51 49 47 45 43 41 39 37 35 33 31 29 27 25 23 21 19 17 15 13 11 9 7 5 3

Row 1

Key

☐ White
■ Black
☐ Pale pink
■ Mid pink
■ Dark pink
■ Red
■ Yellow
■ Golden Yellow
■ Lavender
■ Purple
■ Pale green
■ Mid green
■ Dark Green
■ Very dark green

PART 6

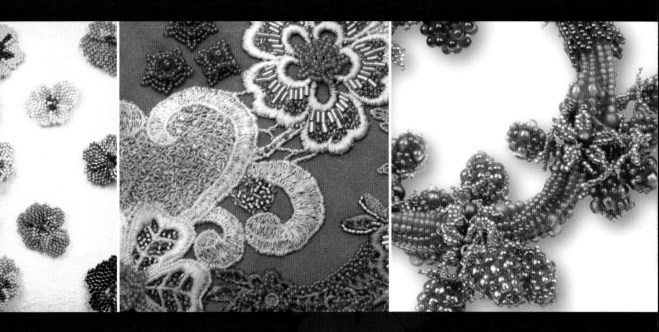

THE ALBUM

On the following pages are examples of our floral beadwork projects that we hope will give
you inspiration for more projects with beaded flowers. Most are self-explanatory as the
flowers could be entirely interchangeable on all sorts of objects and jewellery and clothes.

For some of the examples we have sewn the flowers onto ready-made items
such as tassels, pot pourri bags, cushions and journals. You could of course make the
entire pieces yourself.

Embellish bags and purses with flowery braids and simple flowers.

To make an impact with beaded flowers on soft furnishing,

boxes and books, embellish a piece of embroidery or

flowery material or flat beadwork with

beading and flowers.

Here a flowery braid has been utilised to tie all the different

colours and styles of flower together.

A single flower can be
featured as a centrepiece – either
hanging as a pendant or fixed,
like a button, to a base.

A floral motif can be repeated to
create stunning results.

137

The flowers on this picture frame are stitched on to a beaded trellis which in turn

is stitched on to fabric. You could also use a length of ribbon glued underneath

an object to start beading from.

Tubular flowers make wonderful tassels

and fringes.

To embellish a china candlestick or glass vase, wind strong craft wire around it as a base. Add a length of beaded braid (or, as here, a very long tendril) to which you can stitch your flowers.

These stunning beaded tiaras are actually very simple to create provided you have a deep wire base to start with. They are made by wrapping a beaded braid around the wire base and then embellishing with beaded flowers and crystals.

INDEX

ACKNOWLEDGEMENTS

Thanks to Joyce Mason for being so in tune with our ideas and for designing
a beautiful book (with such good grace whilst under extreme time pressure) which
enhances our style; Claire Crouchley for designing, beading and graphing
the two lovely pictures; Helga Brown, Ann Morton and Brenda Wright for lots
of beading help; and Helen Sherborne for her watercolours.

Also a special thanks to all those beaders who have taken classes with us,
and helped to check our instructions and provide us with endless encouragement.

Photographers' credits:
56 Molka *(Tulip)*; 58 Micko *(Fuchsias)*; 60 Claucarlsen *(Daffodil)*; 62 Elen *(Cornflower)*;
64 Kmitu *(Iris)*; 66 Pamelajane *(Snowdrops)*; 69 Johnsfon *(Pink)*; 72 Atomicrob *(Peony)*;
74 Bedo *(Orchid)*; 76 Iahulbak *(Columbine)*; 124 Juburg *(Anemone)*